ACT NOW!

A Simple Guide to Take Action on Your Greatest Goals and Dreams

Regeanie Corona & Dr. Natalie Phillips

FINN-PHYLLIS
PRESS

Copyright © 2020 by Regeanie Corona and Natalie Phillips

Published by Finn-Phyllis Press, Inc.

All rights reserved. Printed in the United States. No part of this publication may be reproduced, distributed or transmitted in any form or by any means, electronic or mechanical, including photocopying, recording, or by any information storage and retrieval system now known or hereafter invented, without prior written permission from the publisher.

Act Now! / Regeanie Corona and Natalie Phillips -- 1st ed.

ISBN 978-1-7344043-8-8 (pbk)
ISBN 978-1-7344043-9-5 (eBook)

We believe that ACTing now allows each of us to have a greater impact in the world. We want to be an example of that and are therefore dedicated to donating fifty percent of the net profit from sales of this book to a different non-profit organization on an annual basis. We want to have a multiplied impact in our lifetime, and this is one way to do that. So, please know that you are supporting not only this book but also the ripple effect that it can have! We are thankful for your help in this movement to help people who are willing to move past their emotions and boldly step into who they were born to be!

PRAISE FOR ACT NOW!

"Regeanie and Natalie take their own stories of challenges and wins to inspire you to take action by embracing your unique journey and breaking down the doors of fear and self-doubt. This is truly a playbook to help you get yourself in the game!"
—*Dr. Jen Welter, First Female Coach in the NFL and Madden, First Female RB Pro Football, 2X Team USA Gold Medalist*

"We all experience seasons in our lives where we are stopped in our tracks and find ourselves living in neutral. If you need encouragement to push through and re-fire your life, you definitely want to read *ACT Now!*"
—*Sharon Lechter, author of Think and Grow Rich for Women and co-author of New York Times #1 bestseller, Rich Dad Poor Dad*

"What if you had a map that provided step-by-step directions to where you dream of being in three, five, or ten years? What if the map was the same one used by famous innovators like Elon Musk, Oprah Winfrey and Richard Branson? *ACT Now* is this map."
—*Mike Maddock, Serial Entrepreneur, Bestselling Author, Global Keynote Speaker, Growth Strategy Coach, and Re-Invention Expert*

"It is impossible to get through this book and *not* make an inspired first step toward the action required to take vital steps towards realizing and celebrating your authentic journey. As a serial entrepreneur who feels like she's seen everything under the sun when it comes to building a vision, I was shocked by how many times I found myself taking copious notes and celebrating the 'Oh, that's so good' content shared within these pages."
—*Cherie B. Mathews, Founder and CEO of Heal in Comfort*

"A fantastic read! If you want to make a change, be the change, and learn how to transform your life through ACTION, this is the book for you!"
Joni Young, Business Expert and Bestselling Author

"Rarely do I find a book that mirrors my beliefs and actions to truly make things happen! Bravo to these amazing ladies who took real life experiences and challenges and created their own action to make the moves. *ACT Now* is a must read!"
Holly Dowling, Award-winning Global Speaker, Inspirational Thought Leader, Author, Host of "A Celebration of You!" Podcast

"*ACT Now!* is not your ordinary book outlining strategies for success. It is a labor of love and beautiful collaboration between two talented influencers, Regeanie Corona and Dr. Natalie Phillips. I highly recommend

this book as an outstanding guideline for successful personal growth."
—*Dr. Emily Letran, DDS, MS, International Speaker, Certified High-Performance Coach*

"The framework flows well from the authors' origin stories to a simple guide that will change your mindset to one of strategic action. If you're looking for a book that will help you set goals, hold yourself accountable, and make the necessary changes to your life, this is the book for you!"
—*Dr. Amit Gosalia, Board Certified Audiologist, International Speaker, Business Consultant*

To my Father God, thank you for placing a burning desire in my heart to write. To my husband and children (all of them), thank you for making the sacrifice to allow me to create and live out the dreams in my heart. You ALWAYS support everything that I do, and you never judge me on the things that fail. And finally, to all of those who are waiting until "tomorrow" to take action on the dreams in your heart: Tomorrow is not guaranteed, and the world needs to experience what you have to offer. Let go of your fears, take flight, and soar. Your action now can be the inspiration for someone else's tomorrow.

—Regeanie Corona

To my husband, Jason, and my kids, Noa and Makena, I am so thankful for the love, support, encouragement, and patience through this time and focus to make this book happen. I want you to know that everyone has a story to tell. Embrace whatever journey unfolds, and trust that God's plan is always the right plan. He gives you what you can handle, and He provides people in your life and avenues of opportunity for you to succeed if you continue to walk in faith and trust in Him. Be open. Be connected. Be willing to share your unique journey. You never know what one simple ACT can do to inspire and impact the next person.

—Natalie Phillips

CONTENTS

Natalie's Story 1

Regeanie's Story 6

I Believe I Can Fly (Mindset) 15

Jump In; The Water is Fine (Fear) 41

Remove Your Blinders (Self-Worth/Value) 81

The Aha Moments (Epiphanies) 111

It's So Hard to Say Goodbye (Change) 123

Doing What It Takes (Commitment) 141

Just Do It…NOW! (Discipline) 157

I Ain't Tryin' to Be a Goal Digger (Goal Setting) 171

Partners in Crime (Accountability) 187

Take Me to Your Master (Masterminds) 201

Healthy Choices Lead to a Healthy You (Boundaries) ...213

Be Still and Know (Mindfulness) 259

Closing 273

INTRODUCTION

NATALIE'S STORY

Where do I start when it comes to explaining my incredible friendship with Regeanie "Reg" Corona? I know exactly where: January 16, 2016.

We were attending a professional weekend with 100 female business owners and entrepreneurs. Many women had start-ups, many were successful in their businesses and/or non-profit organizations, and many served as mentors. Each day we spent time turning in to the women at our own tables as we went around the circle with an "ask" and a "give." As we each had time to share where we were in our own journeys of entrepreneurship, we were able to ask for help and while listening and offering help from our own strengths and connections.

By completely divine intervention, as Reg would say, I sat at her table each day. Even on the second day, when we were to shuffle and sit by new people, we ended up at the same table. I definitely felt like spending two days in a row at the same table was no accident.

Many things were going on in my mind, as this was one of the first "investments" I'd made into myself other than the education costs (getting my doctorate) to acquire my current "day-job" as an audiologist. Although I was a global ambassador for a female entrepreneurship group, I had not yet fully stepped into my purpose at that time.

In order to attend the event, we had to submit an entry to be placed in the "look book" so that others in attendance could get to know a bit about who we were and what we did. I submitted a quick bio about myself and a new idea I was kicking around that involved how I could possibly help female entrepreneurs. But, even as I arrived, I was stuck in the pattern of introducing myself as "just an audiologist." I was able to maneuver and understand social media channels and knew how to connect people using social media both while at the event and following it, but I was not fully aware that that skill was unique and special, and one that others would be interested in learning about.

In addition, I was coming out of a situation wherein I'd been treated terribly by a female professional and friend (at the time). I had placed my trust in this friendship and professional relationship for the past six or seven years, which in a few unhealthy, childlike, and one-sided transactions behind closed doors blew me entirely out of the water. Through behaving in a way completely opposite to that which this woman promotes, the mean nature, bullying, and confidence-destroying tactics made me believe that no woman could ever support another and that women simply could not be in business together.

There were three things that happened on that first day that softened the hard shell that I had developed after my recent experience:

First, as we focused in on the members of our table to share our stories and do our "ask" and "give," I remember observing the giving nature and plethora of resources and services flying around the table to help each woman until it was the next woman's turn. It was something I had never before seen. I remember Reg introducing herself, and not only was I intrigued by what she did in her business, but I felt a peace surround me as I listened to her giving nature in serving and helping the other women at the table. I said in my head, "I need to make sure I keep in touch with her."

Second, when it was time to meet with a mentor, I took a step back and allowed the other women to choose first. I figured that I would definitely learn from whomever I partnered with, but my idea was still just that—an idea on paper. I didn't feel like I had anything to talk about. I knew exactly which mentor I wanted to talk to, but I didn't take action. The Executive Director of the group walked up to me to ask who I wanted to sit with, and I quickly responded that I would let the others have their chance to choose first. She carefully reminded me that I was just as important, and she encouraged me to let her know who I wanted to speak to so that she could make it happen. I blurted out the name of the one person I wanted to meet in order to learn about who she was and what she was doing. That person was my now dear friend and keynote speaker, Holly Dowling. She was on her way out the door to catch a plane but said she would give me thirty minutes. She will laugh if she reads this because I was so nervous that I don't even remember what I told her about myself or the questions I had for her. In those thirty minutes, many other women saw that she was still in the hotel and tried to sneak in on our time together, but she kept her attention focused on me and never broke eye contact. This alone helped to break down the wall that I'd brought with me to a weekend devoted to women supporting women.

The last thing that happened on this day brought me to tears. At the end of the day, a fierce and successful businesswoman stood up at her table and transparently shared about being torn down. It brings me to tears just thinking about this pivotal moment because this strong woman was demolished, just like I was. She was successful, and yet she too had been hurt. She stood up to thank the women she had met during the day for changing her mind on the ways that women can support other women. I vividly remember tearing up uncontrollably because right there in the same room was another woman, exactly—and yet not exactly—like me.

After the second day, we enjoyed a nice evening out together for dinner, music, and dancing. Reg and I sat together that night and talked. We talked a lot. We talked about our lives, our families, and our businesses. There was one moment when I said that we needed to stay in touch, and she replied "Yes! But, I am terrible at keeping in touch." I quickly answered, "Well, then you are in luck, because I am good at it." I knew from that moment that I had introduced the precedent of being intentional in keeping my word because I wanted to keep this special connection forever. We both got up and danced the night away, and the rest is history.

REGEANIE'S STORY

I love reading Nat's version of our "meet-up" story; it always brings back amazing memories and reminds me that you never know who you will meet at a conference, meeting, or business event if you open yourself up to the opportunity. Sometimes we discover individuals who become more than just another business acquaintance. We find life-long friends and business allies, and they become people to whom we want to stay connected for a lifetime. I used to hear of people who had this experience, yet it didn't quite resonate with me because it had never happened to me. Until, that is, that fateful day in January 2016 when I met Natalie Phillips, whom I lovingly refer to as "Nat."

I had gone to three different self- and business-development conferences in the span of three months. I had traveled to Miami, back to California, and then headed to San Antonio, Texas for a women's conference. I remember that I felt especially compelled to attend this particular event, even though I knew no one personally who would be attending. I was a little uncomfortable because I don't usually go to events where I don't know anyone, but I knew that I needed to be there. Besides, I seemed to be operating in a pattern because, at the other two events that I'd just attended, I didn't know anyone either. I have a very strong faith in God, and I believe that my intuition guides me to the events, activities, and people I am meant to encounter as I live out my life's purpose and journey. There was no doubt in my mind about going, only about what the experience would be like.

As fate would have it, I sat at the same table as Nat. I remember looking at her and thinking that she had such a beautiful smile. It was a warm and friendly smile, and it instantly made me feel comfortable around her. As we went around the table and introduced ourselves, I felt a warmth from her that instantly drew me in and felt familiar.

The next day, we switched tables and had new table partners, allowing us each the opportunity to expand our network and connections, and share our work so that others might offer assistance in helping us with an "ask" that we presented. It was a little like peer coaching meets speed dating. Once again, Nat and I landed at the same table. I remember thinking that I was happy to have her at the same table again because it would give us a little more time to "connect" on a deeper level. I really value genuine connection opportunities versus more typical networking exercises, which often leave me filling unfulfilled, awkward, and bit "icky."

Needless to say, when everyone came together for a final night of fun, dinner, and dancing, Nat and I found each other in the crowd and walked to the venue together, talking and sharing more about ourselves the entire time. When we arrived at the venue, we sat together and continued to share more about our businesses, backgrounds, personal lives, and even our challenges.

I remember Nat telling me that night about another female who had verbally torn her down and subtracted energy from her as she was just beginning to spread her wings and explore how to turn what she loved—using social media platforms as a way to build meaningful connections—into an actual business venture. I also remember feeling very upset and protective, thinking to myself, "How dare another female rain on her parade and try to discourage her from doing something that clearly brings her joy, and as best I can tell, she's actually good at!" This experience had such a negative impact on Nat that she had lost confidence in monetizing her skills and interest, and it relegated her to thinking that maybe she needed to stick to only following her professional path as an audiologist.

Rather than add fuel to this horrible situation, I decided not to focus on the other woman and her shortcomings. Instead, I wanted to focus on giving Nat words of encouragement and nurturing her back to a place of confidence in her skills, regardless of what another person had said to her. I provided feedback and advice on how she could and should handle the negative energy of the other female, and I encouraged her to continue pursuing what she loved and never let another person's opinion sway her from something she feels genuinely purposed to do.

As I had done on so many other occasions, I shared my contact information with Nat, but this time, as she mentioned in her intro, I also gave a disclaimer. I told her, "I'm usually terrible at reaching out and staying in contact with people I meet." One of the reasons why I love her so much is the intentionality that she puts into staying committed to the connections that she makes. She told me, "That's okay. I'm really good at staying in touch." She flashed her beautiful smile, and somehow, I knew that God had provided a genuine connection that would be in my life for a long time to come. I truly believe that it was a divine connection, and I'm thankful that I was open to recognize and receive it.

And the rest, as she said, is history. We have jumped on planes to show up and support each other in person; we have spent countless hours on phone calls and video meetings; we pray for each other; we support each other's family activities; we cheer each other on; we are honest with each other; we have cried and laughed together; and this year, we committed to keep each other accountable to our dreams and desires.

***

So, how did the idea for this book, the two of us starting a business together, and then creating a movement to ignite and inspire others to take action begin?

We both have been choosing a word of the year and have tried to keep each other accountable. In December of 2018, we met for breakfast and each of us was ready to share our words for 2019. Lo and behold, *both* of our words of the year were…ACTION!

We quickly decided that we *had* to make sure we really took action and talked about what it meant to do that. We agreed to keep a standing accountability call, possibly start a mastermind, and even attend a conference each year that would take us both outside of our comfort zones. We did it all and then some, and that's how *ACT Now*! came to be.

Now, it's time for YOU to act!

We don't want you to just read through this book. We want to encourage you to TAKE ACTION on your thoughts, your ideas, and any takeaways that may be stimulated. Grab a pencil, a pen, or a highlighter. Mark up this book. Use Post-it Notes or tabs. Just ACT! We have been so inspired by being focused on taking action all year long, and this book is intended to be used as a guide to help you take *your* next step.

The ACT 3-Step System: Assess-Commit-Transform

We're here to help you to develop your "take action" muscles using our simple three-step system:

- Assess where you are currently
- Commit to where you desire to be
- Transform through the actions of goal setting and accountability

Our hope is that you will get the results you desire by faithfully reading this book, following the ACT system, and connecting with an accountability community and/or partner.

At the end of each chapter, we want you to ACT. Start by writing down the date of your thoughts. Then, after reading each chapter, you will spend time:

A: Assessing how you will take action based on the chapter's topic.

C: Committing by writing down the action you are willing to commit to in the next twelve months.

T: Transforming your life through action by identifying a goal that will transform your identified commitment into a measurable result.

That's it! If you commit to filling out the ACT portion at the end of each chapter, you will build a small but mighty plan of action that you can work on with your accountability partner in order to stay on track.

Every time you think of procrastinating, being inconsistent, or falling into bad habits and negative patterns that prevent you from moving forward, we want you to be reminded to take action instead. Taking action by utilizing this process will take you further than you ever imagined when it comes to accomplishing your goals and dreams. This is the exact process we used for a full year, and our results skyrocketed. You and only you are 100 percent responsible for and accountable to your results. No one can achieve and live your dreams for you, but with the help of this book and an accountability partner, you can achieve your goals. You can achieve the results you desire and finally start confidently living the life of your dreams.

As we went through the process of writing and editing this book, the world began facing a very difficult and challenging time due to the COVID-19 pandemic. This unprecedented time has caused physical, emotional, and economic devastation around the world. As of the time of this writing, more than twenty million infections have occurred worldwide along with more than 740,000 deaths. To make matters worse, society as a whole is incredibly split when it comes to their perspective on the virus. In some places, such as the United States—in the midst of a presidential election year, no less—the topic of the virus and the recommendations to lower the spread have become extremely politicized and polarizing. Whatever your views may be on the virus, however, we believe that there is one thing we can all agree on, and that is the importance, now more than ever, of taking intentional steps toward your dreams and goals. A certain future is never guaranteed to any of us, but the way we act upon that which we value and believe to be important can become our North Star in the midst of chaos and uncertainty.

Our desire is to spark a movement and inspire people around the world to stop waiting to take action when it comes to what's important to them. We understand that there are many layers of challenges that can stop someone from taking action. Maybe it's a fear of failing or a fear of succeeding or even a fear of the responsibilities that might come with success. Maybe it's a resistance to embarking on a significant change, including a total shift in mindset. Maybe it's a perceived barrier such as low access to resources. Whatever the reason, we hope that this book and exposure to our own individual journeys (and even our own inner battles) will help to inspire and motivate you to stop waiting for tomorrow to take action on the dreams in your heart and the goals that will help you realize them.

CHAPTER ONE

I BELIEVE I CAN FLY (MINDSET)

"Your beliefs become your thoughts, your thoughts become your words, your words become your actions, your actions become your habits, your habits become your values, your values become your destiny."
—Ghandhi

What do you believe about yourself? Do your beliefs play a role in your ability to take action on your life's desires and dreams?

Your beliefs, and what you hold to be essential in life, are critical components of your overall mindset. What you believe about yourself and those things that you find valuable (your values) definitely play a role in whether or not you are confident enough to make things happen in your life by taking action.

A belief is an idea that a person reveres as a truth.

It is viewed as a reality, whether or not it is actually true. When we believe in something, we have faith and trust that it is so and thereby begin to have confidence in it. Beliefs help shape our very existence as human beings. They are developed from different sources, including what other people say, how we were raised, our experiences, and even the cultural and societal influences to which each of us is exposed. A belief remains with a person until something happens to cause them to reevaluate and/or change that belief.

Values are the beliefs that we hold necessary in everyday life. They become the standards by which we live our lives and to which we are committed. Values help us to make decisions, choose who we will interact with, and often guide the way we set goals and take action toward those goals.

As we grow and develop, our values, beliefs, and priorities shift based on what we experience in life and the result of those experiences. When we allow our values to guide our decisions, we focus on what is important to us, and doing so generally fosters a sense of well-being. Together, our beliefs and values contribute to our attitudes and overall human behavior.

Because our beliefs are central to who we are and the way we live our lives, it stands to reason that they are also a critical component of our mindset, defining who we are. While beliefs can be self-sustaining and empowering, they can also be extremely limiting. Beliefs that limit us, also referred to as self-limiting beliefs, are those beliefs that prevent or restrict us from living our lives to our fullest potential. Limiting beliefs influence behavior and can lead to debilitating patterns. If you're going to stop them from impacting your life, you need to be aware of them. Once you can identify them, it becomes essential to reframe the limiting beliefs and replace them with empowering ones. Ultimately, you can train yourself to change the actions you take based on limiting beliefs and reverse the predictable results that you have received time and time again.

How often do we find ourselves stuck, unable to move forward on something that we know is important, simply because we are fixed in a specific mindset that suggests that our options are limited? This fixed mindset keeps us from living up to our fullest potential and causes us not to pursue the dreams in our hearts. Together, we have had numerous discussions about the impact of a person's mindset on their ability to drive outcomes and results. This includes understanding how limiting beliefs can prevent us from taking action toward the goals that we desire to achieve.

We believe it is vitally important to acknowledge that our ability to have success in accomplishing our dreams starts with understanding our mindset. Looking at the various areas of our mindset that contribute to the overall ability to establish goals and succeed in accomplishing those goals can assist us in putting the necessary actions in place to lead to goal achievement and personal success.

REGEANIE'S STORY

I remember my first trip to Colorado to visit Natalie. As she was driving me to the airport for my departure, we had a fascinating conversation that will stay with me forever. It had everything to do with mindset. As we discussed entrepreneurship, Nat said that she really wanted to start a business but didn't feel like she could because she "went to school for and studied to become an audiologist." Since this was what she was educated to do, it was as though she believed that somehow her chosen "profession" disqualified her from having the experience and/or expertise to succeed in another industry. Of course, this couldn't have been further from the truth, but her mindset at the time kept her fixed in this belief—a belief that limited her ability to take action on something that, deep inside, she desired to pursue.

After having a dialog about it for almost an hour, she experienced a mindset shift. A false belief that held her back was broken, and that break would transform her forever. It was a transformation that opened the door of opportunity and possibility, and signaled that she had permission to be more and do more than what her professional degrees "allowed."

Our mindset can literally keep us stuck and prevent us from moving forward on just about anything. The perspective that we choose to apply to a particular situation can make the difference between maintaining a positive outlook and developing a negative outlook (and vice versa). This perspective can be game-changing. It can make the difference between realizing success in life or not.

For as long as I can remember, I have been a positive person. I've seen the glass not just as half full but as completely full, no matter the circumstances. I never knew exactly why I innately gravitated toward this mindset, but I know that it had something to do with one simple fact that I embraced very early in my life: "We can choose to be joyful, or we can choose to be miserable."

My favorite person in my young, six-year-old life, my Aunt Maxine, died of cancer, and no one could look me in the eyes and explain what happened to her. Everyone was avoiding the responsibility of telling me that she had left and was never coming back. I couldn't comprehend the concept of death at that time. My brain was simply too immature. All I knew was that someone I loved very much, and who had been instrumental in the first few years of my life, was gone forever. This was the first experience in my life that led to a conscious decision to choose to view life positively, even when it hurt.

I was devastated by this loss. She was my aunt, my friend, my playmate, my biggest fan, and my greatest protector. I can vividly remember looking at her body in the open casket at the funeral home and thinking, "She's just asleep, and I'll see her tomorrow." When I realized that there would be no tomorrow or time together in the future, I felt abandoned. How could she leave me? After a few days of feeling simply awful, I implemented what I believe was my first life motto and protection mechanism. I told myself that since things and people can come and go, I could not place my trust and joy in those things. I decided at the age of six that I would choose to be positive in every circumstance, even if I really wanted to feel something different.

Throughout my life, I maintained this uncanny way of looking at every situation, especially death and loss, as a part of life, and while it might hurt, I would still choose positivity as my leading emotion. This belief system carried me for many years and through numerous negative experiences. Until one day, it was as though I'd lost connection with all that I had believed in. Joy was replaced with complaining, negativity, and constant negative self-talk. I was going through a divorce (a choice made by me), co-parenting while raising two small children, and watching everything around me fall apart. I had always been a person who could control my emotions and the way they impacted me. But not anymore.

Even though I had a great job and was making six figures annually, my finances were in ruins as a result of bad choices and the divorce. I felt horrible about myself and what I was putting my children through, and worse, I felt like I had lost all control of everything. The devastation was even bleeding over into my work life. Rumors were swarming in the office about my circumstances, and people were whispering in corners as I walked by, looking at me as though I had suddenly turned neon pink.

I remember having a friend come to my office to talk to me and share that our leadership was concerned about my "current state." What the heck? My current state was that I was going through a challenging time as I was trying to adjust to living life as a divorced, single, financially devastated mother.

I had a career in the still male-dominated field of Information Technology and Cyber Security, and even though I was in senior management, my male counterparts and mostly male leaders looked at me as though I was suddenly less capable than I had been all the years before. They saw me as irrational, moody, irritable, no longer a team player, and undependable. It didn't matter that I was still producing the same level of work output, managing my staff effectively, and juggling multiple multi-million-dollar projects in the same way I had before. All that was seen was my shift in "mindset."

"What you focus on becomes your reality!" I certainly didn't coin this phrase, as it has been said by many people in many different ways with the same underlying meaning: The mind is powerful, and it has the ability to manifest into reality what it continually thinks about. This principle became all too real for me during this challenging time in my life. I was focused on everything that was wrong, everything that I didn't have, everything that was out of my control, and the misery it was causing in my life. Guess what? My choice to focus on the negative was also drawing more negative into my atmosphere.

It wasn't until I took a step back one day to examine why things were going so woefully wrong that I finally had a moment of clarity. I was forced into this level of self-examination after landing in the ER with a racing heart and all of the symptoms of a heart attack. After several hours hooked up to monitors, blood work, and a series of other tests, I was told that I was perfectly healthy and had experienced an anxiety attack. I was referred to a therapist whom I met once, and in that one session, I had a profound revelation: I didn't need a therapist to tell me how to address this issue. Don't get me wrong, therapists play a vital role in helping individuals move past emotional challenges, but for me, at that particular moment, therapy wasn't what I needed. I already knew exactly what I needed, but I had to have a "perceived" life-threatening event in order to be reminded of it. I needed to get back to making a conscious decision to

CHOOSE positivity and joy.

I would love to say that I was able to simply overcome negative thinking, but that's not what happened. It took a few months of sincere prayer, self-assessment, and positive self-talk to lead me back to a mindset focused on growth, joy, and peace. But the experience of choosing to lead with negativity reminded me just how powerful the mind and its thoughts are.

Your mindset is literally a game-changer. It will determine how successful you are at living a fulfilled life and reaching your dreams, or it will paralyze you and destroy those dreams.

I have experienced many obstacles and challenges in my lifetime, some of which I felt as though I would never recover from or make it through. Besides loss, my earliest memories of some of the challenges I faced are from times when I was a young girl, trying to sort through my identity as a fair-skinned African American who didn't quite fit in (I later found out that I was adopted and of mixed ethnicity, which explained a great deal). I was teased and bullied by other African American children who I grew up with and was called nasty names based on the fair tone of my skin and the length/texture of my hair. It didn't help that I looked nothing like either of my parents, a reality for which I really had no plausible explanation. There is a saying that I could definitely relate to at that point in my life: "I was too white to be black and too black to be white." What that saying really translates to is a lack of acceptance. It was during these formidable years that I continued to learn the valuable lesson of choosing to look for positive outcomes and lessons in every situation.

While many of these lessons came at a high emotional price, they also paid a high dividend. I was being shaped into a better human, prepared for a life of service and gratitude, and formed by fire into someone who could persevere. I was learning what it meant to develop a growth mindset—a mindset that chooses to look at the glass as half full instead of half empty and to continually visualize the glass as completely full, regardless of how high or low the measuring mark may have been in the moment.

NATALIE'S STORY

I have felt that I was guided into living with a mindset of overcoming and having a positive outlook. However, as it did for Reg, it came in a roundabout way for me. As a child, I constantly observed my parents giving of themselves—to church, to Bible studies, to bringing people into the home who did not have a place to go. With youth groups and other families, we did many things. It was all I knew. But over time, I became critical and more cynical. As a teenager, I wasn't always thankful for the extra people in my home all the time; I wasn't always grateful to share the celebration of my birthday with others. I wasn't proud or happy and felt that it was more of an "obligation" to do things that were planned. My mindset shifted from one of gratitude to one of rolling my eyes back in my head and being disrespectful.

This obligation continued as my longing to feel part of a group put false identities in my head. I believed that people would judge me for what I wore, who I hung out with, or who I went to prom with or dated. The keyword in all of this is "false." The mind is a terrible bully when we feed it with false thoughts and start believing what we are eating.

Over time, I learned how to shift my mindset from "woe is me" and take responsibility for things that happened to me. I had to recognize that I was part of the decision process that led to the undesired outcome. This mindset shift allowed me to be free to take steps (and even leaps) of faith. I was able to accept that when things happen in my life, good or bad, there can always be something positive that comes out of it.

LOOKING AT THE MIND

The mind and the way that it perceives aspects of your life is what creates your frame of mind or mindset. The mind is a potent tool that shapes who you are. Everything starts with thoughts in your mind. Your thoughts are what give you a frame of reference about yourself as well as the world around you. The accumulation of these thoughts is what is referred to as your mindset, and it is this mindset that will determine how you view life's situations, including whether or not you perceive situations as opportunities or challenges. Your mindset can either limit you or propel you.

As a matter of fact, the mind was an important enough topic to be mentioned ninety-two times in the Bible. References were made to the way a person thinks and the power that her thoughts could have. Your thoughts are what determine your experiences. This truth serves as the premise of all spiritual texts and esoteric schools of thought, and it is reflected in many scientific spheres, such as quantum mechanics.

People have specific thought patterns that they picked up from society, their parents, or groups and organizations. They then project these thought patterns out to their surroundings and may mistakenly believe that their own projections and interpretations are the "truth." The truth may be different from person to person, depending on their thoughts. This is where diversity emanates!

LOOKING AT OUR THOUGHTS

There's a great quote from Napoleon Hill on thoughts. It says, "Remember that your dominating thoughts attract, through a definite law of nature, by the shortest and most convenient route, their physical counterpart. Be careful what your thoughts dwell upon." The human mind is magnificently creative.

Everything starts with a thought. We are able to create anything that our minds can conceive of, so it stands to reason that creativity is not bound by positive or negative results; it simply exists to manifest thoughts into reality irrespective of the impending result. This means that we should be aware of our thoughts and how we utilize them.

Consider our inner critic. It lives with us 24/7, and it often contributes to our negative perceptions of ourselves. We talk to ourselves constantly throughout the day through our sub-conscious thoughts, also known as our inner critic. Some researchers have noted that most people talk to themselves around 50,000 times a day. Unfortunately, according to a 2013 Psychology Today article, the vast majority of those internal conversations, up to seventy percent, are negative. Imagine the cumulative impact that these toxic conversations have had on you over time—and continue to have.

It's time to set your inner critic straight by replacing the negative conversations with ones that support your goals and dreams. We are not suggesting that you constantly affirm positivity in every thought; while that is helpful in the short-term, it isn't sustainable. Instead, we suggest that you use this book to help you identify what is important to you, develop a realistic plan to pursue what is important, and develop a habit of supportive internal conversations that can help you to stay on track and remain positive about your pursuits.

THE IMPORTANCE OF MINDSET

If our mindset is the collection of thoughts and beliefs that influence the way that we view and live our lives, it stands to reason that our mindset also dictates how we respond to any given situation. Both internal (genetics) and external (experiences, backgrounds, etc.) factors combine to contribute to the way we react to a situation.

Life is guaranteed to present challenges. You cannot go through the human experience without experiencing some level of difficulty. It is during these challenging times that a positive and focused mindset allows you not only to overcome the obstacles but even to welcome them as opportunities from which you can learn and grow.

Having the right mindset is critical to living a joyful life. Regardless of who you are or what you do, you need the right mindset to achieve success in life. For example, people who believe their abilities can be improved through hard work and dedication typically move ahead and succeed by taking action without excuses. These same people also demonstrate that they are willing to learn and are most successful in different aspects of their life.

HOW MINDSET DEVELOPS

For most of us, our mindsets are created at an early

age. As we grow and mature, life experiences and events can contradict our prior knowledge and change our mindsets. However, childhood knowledge continues to remain with us and becomes our reference point for much of our lives.

While repetition plays a vital role in the creation of our habits and beliefs, our emotions also factor into the equation. When repeated thoughts and actions are mixed with emotions, results can change. Both good and bad habits are formed through repetition, but the practice can become embedded more rapidly and with greater conviction when those habits are combined with emotion.

As our mindset continues to develop, we often continue to repeat and practice the beliefs that were formed in our early childhood. If our mindset is fixed, we tend to mature with self-limiting beliefs that become hard to shed. People who have fixed mindsets believe that their traits are a given and can't be changed. These individuals are always concerned with being "good enough" and whether or not they have what it takes to be successful.

THE DANGERS OF A FIXED MINDSET

While the advantages of a growth mindset may seem evident to many, they continue to operate with a fixed mindset nonetheless. This can prevent them from having success in their lives because they are unable to develop the critical skills needed for growth. This limitation often sabotages their ability to experience real joy and well-being in their lives. See if you recognize any of these fixed mindset traits in yourself or someone you know:

- The obsession to prove worth
- Perfectionism
- The need for constant validation
- Devaluing the importance of effort

At a high level, here is how someone with a fixed mindset looks at things:

Skills: The fixed mindset believes skills are something you're born with, and they can't be changed.

Challenges: The fixed mindset regards challenge as something to avoid at all costs. There is a constant threat that a problem could expose your lack of skill, and you tend to give up quickly when in these circumstances.

Effort: Effort is considered unnecessary by the fixed mindset. It's something that people resort to only when they aren't **good enough** for the job.

Feedback: Feedback puts the fixed mindset on the defensive. When given feedback, people with a fixed mindset take it personally and consider it an exclusive attack on their performance or skills. If it isn't to their liking, they may even ignore the feedback completely.

Setbacks: When faced with setbacks, people with a fixed mindset will shift the blame to others. They also get discouraged easily and are more likely to quit altogether.

REGEANIE'S STORY

Though I mastered the art of being positive, I still experienced some effects of a fixed mindset. Because I was bullied as a child and often not accepted, I grew up feeling as though I wasn't enough. This feeling of inadequacy led me to believe that if I could just prove my worth to those I encountered, they would see that I was likable and worthy.

I became a perfectionist and a people pleaser, always seeking the approval of others. Outwardly I appeared confident, but internally I wanted others to like and accept me. I was a ball of low self-esteem. These feelings of inadequacy followed me well into adulthood and resulted in decisions that didn't align with my values, directing time and energy toward things that were not important to my higher purpose. It wasn't until I began to learn about and consciously work toward a growth mindset that I began to overcome the need to please others, especially at my own expense.

THE POWER OF A GROWTH MINDSET

Let's examine a growth mindset and how powerful it is. A growth mindset allows people to view themselves as capable of doing well in most—if not all—situations. People with a growth mindset definitely don't consider themselves to be restricted by their abilities or even their circumstances. They choose to believe that they can do whatever they've set their minds to doing, as long as they practice. This optimism and creativity indicate a growth mindset and often leads to someone who:

- Improves through effort
- Offers a sense of fulfillment
- Develops resilience
- Buffers against demotivation
- Encourages perseverance
- Promotes critical thinking
- Creates a "practice makes perfect" viewpoint

In contrast to a fixed mindset, here's how a growth mindset perceives things:

Skills: The growth mindset believes that skills are something that you can continuously change, improve, and develop. Skills come from hard work, so you can't stop working.

Challenges: The growth mindset is eager to embrace challenges and views them as an opportunity to grow. The chance to engage in a challenge makes the growth mind more persistent.

Effort: Effort is essential for a growth mindset and may even override talent. When the growth mindset sees the effort as the path to success, it realizes the necessity for lifelong learning.

Feedback: The growth mindset views feedback as something constructive and an experience to learn from. It is an effective means by which to identify areas that need improvement.

Setbacks: Instead of putting being seen as negative experiences, setbacks and failures are seen as stepping-stones to success. They are ways to improve on current talents and efforts, and present as infinite growing opportunities.

CAN YOU CHANGE YOUR MINDSET?

Absolutely! Beliefs can be changed when they no longer serve you or enable you to reach your goals. Ways to change one's mindset include:

- Resisting change
- Using fear to change your mindset
- Using actions to change your mindset

- Identifying your counter mindsets
- Shifting gears from the negative to the positive
- Understand WHY you need to change
- Starting small to finish big

STRATEGIES TO DEVELOP A GROWTH MINDSET

When you let results such as your test scores, your weight, your job, or your appearance define you, you become the victim of a fixed mindset. On the contrary, a growth mindset is all about learning, and you can speed up the process by following some true and tried strategies, including:

- Engaging in continual learning
- Being committed
- Developing healthy self-esteem
- Working on your perspective
- Setting effective goals
- Managing your inner negative voice
- Facing adversity
- Being open to feedback

DEALING WITH INEVITABLE SETBACKS

After debating the good and the bad aspects of different mindsets, it becomes clearer that the way the mind responds to setbacks, disappointments, or failure is very important.

For instance, with a fixed mindset, a setback becomes a failure that distorts reality. This distorted view prevents people from seeing a situation for what it is. And, without a clear picture of the situation, it can become impossible to pivot, solve, or make any progress on that situation.

But, with a growth mindset, this setback doesn't become overwhelming. In fact, it is often seen as something that will redirect your efforts in the right direction.

Consider some examples of situations that may be viewed as negative, but with a growth mindset applied, can be reframed for positive and growth-filled outcomes:

- The importance of failure
- Experience and knowledge
- Resilience and growth
- Change your strategy
- Seeking inspiration through others
- Using failure as leverage
- Redefining priorities and values
- Don't let your failure define you
- Helps reach your potential
- Failure is always better than regret
- Setbacks yield a sense of direction

UNDERSTANDING THE THREE BRAINS

In addition to understanding the importance of mindset, there is also value in understanding the physiology of our brain and how it impacts our mindset. To help you understand thoughts a bit more, we need to examine the three regions of the brain: reptilian, limbic, and rational. These three parts of the brain are continually working to co-exist.

The reptilian brain, also called the "lizard" or "crocodile" brain, is concerned only with primitive survival. It focuses on basic survival needs such as food, shelter, safety, and procreation. Further, it is the area of the brain that causes us to feel fear, whether real or imagined. Since it is concerned with our safety, the reptilian brain is going to do everything it can to control situations and ensure that you do not feel fear. This means that if it believes your actions will put you in danger (real or imagined), it will try to prevent you from implementing those actions.

The limbic brain focuses on our emotional existence and how we feel. It is only concerned with our feeling good. If it believes that our actions are in alignment with feeling good, then it is all in. Otherwise, it wants nothing to do with what we are proposing.

The rational brain thrives on and wants anything related to logic, organization, and planning.

As you can imagine, our minds are in a constant conversation across these three regions, and each is fighting to take control. This war between the three regions of the brain is what stops us in our tracks and contributes to us being "stuck." We are stuck as we fear we will be in danger if we take action. We are stuck sometimes making emotional decisions. We are stuck and don't make a decision altogether when we overanalyze and never take action. This physiology of the brain impacts our ability to take action because in its attempt to "protect" us, it impacts our mindset and actually holds us back.

WHERE MIGHT YOU BE STUCK?
- Are you able to identify an area of the brain that may need your awareness and attention?
- Do you have a healthy balance of the regions of the brain, or do you need to focus your attention on developing a growth mindset?

It's TIME to frame your mindset around growth and take action!

Chapter Review

- Beliefs are developed from different sources and stay with us until something happens to cause reevaluation or change.
- Our mindset can keep us stuck and prevent us from moving forward.
- What you focus on becomes your reality.
- Repetition and emotion play important roles in the creation of our habits and beliefs.

- A growth mindset allows people to view themselves as capable of doing well.
- Beliefs can be changed when they no longer serve you or enable you to get to your goals.

Time to ACT!

Today's Date:

Assess – Journal about what you wish to take action on related to this chapter's topic.

Commit – Write down the action you are willing to commit to in the next twelve months.

Transform – Identify an actionable goal that will transform the commitment into a measurable outcome.

CHAPTER TWO

JUMP IN; THE WATER IS FINE (FEAR)

"F-E-A-R has two meanings:
Forget Everything and Run or
Face Everything and Rise.
The choice is yours."

I (Natalie) remember the day, the restaurant, and the table where Reg and I sat down and shared our fears with each other and talked about what was holding us back and what we were afraid of. The ONE thing she told me without pause and with great confidence was that FEAR is there for everyone, but what we *must* do is not avoid it, not go around it, but instead, move *through* it.

What EXACTLY does that mean? Let's step back

to examine where FEAR originates.

There are some aspects we as humans share with "lower" life forms. Like humans, most life forms have a heart, a brain, and lungs. But in the most primal, primitive part of the mind, there lurks a place called the amygdala. In humans, it's about the size of an almond, and its function is to keep us alive long enough to breed. It is present in all mammals (while varying slightly in size), and it serves a very important purpose. Simply put, it tells us what to do when we're in danger. When you hear the phrase "fight-or-flight," it's a reference to the work of the amygdala. There are some wonderful benefits to the amygdala. For example, when something big and loud is coming at you, you're probably running before you even know what it is. The amygdala keeps you alive by pumping adrenaline into your system. What we do with that adrenaline is the reaction that keeps us alive.

Fight or Flight. Are You Going to Face the Enemy? Or Will You Run?

The problem is, what was useful centuries ago has limited use in today's world. After all, this fight-or-flight reaction is built into the deepest, most instinctive part of our brain. But what do we need it for anymore, other than to occasionally compel us to jump back up on the curb when a taxi tries to take us out in the crosswalk?

When you hear yourself saying that something is too risky or too dangerous, and that you *shouldn't do it*, that's the amygdala talking. So, while every activity might not be life or death anymore, having a part of your brain on duty to keep you a little cautious isn't necessarily a bad thing. Except, it is. The worst part of the amygdala is that *everything* goes through it before going to the other parts of the brain. And, while that can be handy when driving--making you more alert to other drivers--or in dark alleys and war zones, it isn't at all helpful when you are looking to make a change outside of your comfort zone or achieve something new. During these times, it simply gets in the way by creating unwarranted fear. That's when you hear "the voice." You know the one. It says things like:

- "That's too risky."
- "It's too dangerous."
- "What if I fail?"
- "What if I go broke?"
- "What about my retirement fund?"
- "It's a pipe dream."
- "Don't take chances!"

What you need to realize is that people who succeed are people who take risks. Period. Believe it or not, people who are rich often lose vast fortunes on the chances they take, but they keep going, and that's where the next risk pays off. You cannot be successful if you continually listen to your amygdala, because you'll always end up giving into your fear. However, our instinct is to run, to flee from risk. Our very being is designed to fight change and run from challenges.

Believe it or not, you can change this. But keep in mind, these reactions are so deeply embedded that they aren't going to change overnight. And they certainly won't change easily. But it CAN be done.

As Nelson Mandela said,

I learned that courage was not the absence of fear, but the triumph over it. The brave man is not he who does not feel afraid, but he who conquers that fear.

That's reprogramming for you! Every time you conquer fear, you put a little reprogramming into the amygdala. Not that you want your fear to go away completely—we still need to have it on duty for those important moments for when we truly *are* in danger. But, we need to listen to it only when we truly need it—when there is real danger ahead.

Only then will we find success.

NATALIE'S STORY

I was fearful of many things, and I am STILL fearful of things.

FEAR is a constant; I don't think we can ever expect to avoid fear altogether. I have a list of fears, and they sound a little like this: "I am fearful of failure; of people judging me; of failing those who depend on me; of debt and not achieving financial freedom; of passing on debt to my children; of my children not finding their own successes in life, including having a healthy money mindset."

But although I acknowledge that I do have fears, I don't let it stop me. I continue to have the dialogue I feed my thoughts and ultimately my actions that "it *has* to get done, so just *do it*", "I want this to happen and in order for it to happen, I have to *move*", "this *will be* better in the long run", and the one that truly makes me push through—"if I don't do this, who loses?"

FEAR can make us pause and become paralyzed. For some, it creates more than a pause; it creates a complete STOP. A negative event can cause a person to "park" and never move from the spot they stopped in. For others, FEAR causes them to be FEAR-LESS and do whatever it is that scares them while they experience the fear. They feel that pushing forward in spite of the fear is better than not taking action. For these people, quitting is not an option.

Our good friend Lisa Copeland, author of *Car Buying, Her Way:The Fierce Girl's Roadmap to the Car of Your Dreams*, co-author of *Crushing Medioc-*

rity: 10 Ways to Rise Above the Status Quo, and President of Austin Mortgage Associates, has always talked to both of us about the importance of putting yourself out there, even if you feel afraid. Actually, it's even more important to put yourself out there if you feel afraid because it is going to force you to confront the very thing that is holding up your progress. This was some of the best advice that each of us ever received, and Lisa has always served as a great model for learning to be FEAR-LESS.

Another friend and mentor, Sharon Lechter, author of *Think and Grow Rich for Women: Using Your Power to Create Success and Significance* said, "Fear, the worst of all enemies, can be effectively cured by forced repetition of acts of courage." The first time we face a fear, it is empowering. To place yourself in circumstances to face fear repeatedly is a *game changer*. We have both been encouraged and inspired by the many books that Sharon has authored, especially the book she was commissioned by the Napoleon Hill Foundation to annotate and help release to the public, *Outwitting The Devil*. This book is all about facing your fears and moving past them to take action.

We are grateful to have had this wisdom imparted on us by amazing mentors and friends who helped us and countless others who refuse to allow fear to stop them from going after their BIG goals and dreams.

THE PROBLEM WITH FEAR

How many times have you looked forward to something that scares you? How often do you think that a frightening situation is going to turn out great? Chances are, unless you really love haunted houses and possibly are an adrenaline junkie, rarely (if ever).

Fear does not have a bright side. Fear does not have a happy ending. Fear will *only* see the downside, the disaster waiting to happen, the pit that opens under your feet. Fear cannot see the success at the end of the journey or the benefits that taking a risk can bring.

Ready to make a speech? What if you mumble?

Ready to go on a date? What if they don't like you?

Ready to get a promotion? What if the new job is too much to handle?

Fear does this. Instead of knowing that you're going to have the audience's rapt attention, or that you might meet that one person you've dreamed of meeting or celebrate that corner office they'll award you, fear will only let you see the pitfall and traps, which grow larger by the minute. Why does fear hold us back? What is it that makes us so afraid?

FEAR IS IMMEDIATE

Remember, everything goes through the amygdala. Everything. Being chased by a rabid wolf? Now is not the time to stop and think too hard about it. Getting one offer on selling your car for half the price you asked? That is an *excellent* time to stop and think things over. But fear won't let you stop and think. The amygdala is designed to make you react quickly. If you're afraid that there will be no more offers for your car, or if you're afraid that there is not going to be another option in work, relationships, or whatever the category may be, there's no option to think things through. Fear screams, "*Act now!*" and often has a result of long-term regret, especially if taking action is rooted and motivated by fear alone.

FEAR KEEPS US FROM LEAVING

Often, animals kept in cages too long—even abused ones—will fight to remain in their cages when finally offered freedom. They understand where they are, and they know what to expect. Whatever lies beyond the small enclosure is too big, too grand and frightening even to consider. It's much the same reason why people will remain in abusive relationships. They'll work relentlessly in dead-end jobs with bad employers, but will stay where they are, with the ill-treatment, because it's familiar to them. Fear of the unknown is often much scarier than the certainty of where we already are. Fear keeps us from leaving, from getting help, from striking out on our own when we can no longer tolerate the life we have. Fear keeps us "safe," even when we are not at all safe. Helen Keller put it this way: "Avoiding danger is no safer in the long run than outright exposure. The fearful are caught as often as the bold." Often the reality is that we are "caught" more often and more quickly if we don't face the fear.

FEAR GIVES US A FALSE SENSE OF COMMUNITY

The same part of the brain that dictates fight or flight also understands that there is safety in numbers. A united group of people can fight a larger enemy than a single person can. In the worst-case-scenario minds of primitive man, maybe the lion would eat someone else, and you could run away. In those days, taking a risk meant the possibility of being outcast from the tribe. Today we still have those "tribes" in which we strive to remain, although they may look a little different than the tribes of old.

What if you make a fool of yourself at work? What if your friends don't like you anymore and don't want you around them? What if your presentation is so bad that you get fired? What if…what if…what if…! Even people who have been married for decades will hesitate to ask for something they want or need for fear their spouse will reject them out-of-hand. "What if she laughs at what I need?"

"What if he thinks I'm a bad person because I asked?" Is it worth asking to find out?

FEARS STOPS US SHORT OF FAILURE

Often, we won't try anything unless we already know we excel at it. Learning to play an instrument, for example, is done in secret, or at the very least, alone. If we can't sit at a piano and play like a master, then it's best to pass it by or wait until we have the privacy needed to make mistakes. Because what if we do fail? What if we fall on our face on the red carpet? Maybe we're all a little paranoid, because in the day and age of social media we're always worried that our terrible mistake could possibly be shared for the world to see. Worse than that, if the mistake is spectacular enough, there's even a chance you could go viral. In that case, you're suddenly the fool, and people will see you as a flawed human being.

We still worry though, don't we? We think, "If at first you can't succeed, it's better not to try." We tend to forget, though, that trying and failing is how we become proficient at something. You cannot play the piano like a master if you don't ever play at all. In our minds we can be perfect and gifted, but training our fingers to hit the right keys in the right order takes time. There are risks required—not to mention a whole lot of practice, private or otherwise. But if fear stops you before you're even out of the gate, you're never going to be able to express yourself in new and wonderful ways.

REGEANIE'S STORY

I have always told myself that the feeling of fear is powerful and if I could use that power as a catalyst to move through the fear then I could be unstoppable in achieving my goals and dreams.

If I told you that I've always been able to use this power to bust through my greatest fears, I'd be lying to you and I wouldn't do that. The truth is, I feel fear over something almost weekly, personal health, finances, achieving my goals, the well-being of my family, the sustainability of my businesses, the state of the world, you name it and it hits me at some point or another. However, over the years I have learned to harness these fears and exploit them.

When I feel fear, my immediate reaction now becomes identifying actions that can I take immediately to counteract the physical and emotional feelings that I am experiencing. Taking action now is how I've trained my brain to respond to fear. I no longer give my fears time to manifest into the monsters that I know they can become. I know that I will never overcome the feelings of fear and I'm at peace with that. I actually believe that fear can protect us when we are in a real and present danger, but as you probably now know very well, most fears are merely a perception of danger and not truly real. Instead of giving in to the fear, I force the fear to give me the energy and motivation needed to take action.

FEAR KEEPS US FROM OURSELVES

If you keep listening to fear, it will eventually prevent you from realizing your potential. Fear would keep you in bed, under the blankets and generally immobile, if it could. Humans cannot grow in such an environment. Muscles unused atrophy and become unusable. It's through putting effort into and pressure on muscles that they develop and strengthen. The five-pound weight you started with during your workout regimen becomes less of a challenge after a while. More weight or more reps must be added to continually challenge the muscle's growth. People are the same way. Through trial and error, stress and pressure, we grow. We fail. Often. That's part of the process. Mark Zuckerberg, founder of Facebook, put it this way: "The biggest risk is not taking any risk.…" In a world that's changing really quickly, the only strategy that is guaranteed to fail is not taking risks." Without risk, we too atrophy.

FEAR THWARTS TRUST

You have intuition. You have instincts. You probably know things without knowing *how* you know them. Have you ever had the experience of meeting someone new and having the strangest feeling that that person was not to be trusted? But, in another situation, you met someone for the first time and within the space of half an hour discovered someone you knew was going to be a pleasant—if not a significant—part of your life from that moment forward. How is it we're able to not only make these kinds of judgments but trust them? As it turns out, there are tell-tale signs of which we're likely unaware in the moment. Small things. The other person's tone of voice, for example, or the amount of eye contact someone gives us tells us worlds about the person we're talking to—if we know what to look for. The good news is, you do. You've spent your entire life in a trial-and-error process that has proven that certain people cannot be trusted, while others can. So, when we see something that subconsciously reminds us of those lessons, our brain translates that into what's generally called a "gut feeling."

Unfortunately, fear often blocks this, and everyone becomes suspect. That person over there is hiding something, even though they're smiling. The person who has never let you down probably hasn't just because they haven't yet had the opportunity to do so. Fear makes unreasonable assumptions that you don't even realize are being made. So, even if that smiling person doesn't necessarily look like a danger, we believe they *could be*. Fear makes us doubt ourselves. Fear puts us off and makes us unsure of our feelings. It makes us double and triple-think every decision, to the point where we're no longer capable of deciding at all.

FEAR MAKES US QUESTION OUR ABILITIES

Fear offers us a nice double whammy. Not only does it convince us that we can't do something, it then sets out to prove it. Being afraid of learning to drive a car means that you will never be comfortable behind the wheel. That, in turn, means that you'll never relax or enjoy the experience. It's tough to excel at things we don't like doing. Fear will lead the way to prove itself right; it's called a self-fulfilling prophecy. Are you afraid of being judged by others? Fear will make that slip in front of people most likely to judge you. Are you afraid of being alone? Fear will isolate you from others. In addition, when we allow ourselves or others to speak fear into our lives, we start believing the spoken word. So much so that we need to be careful we are not investing into this self-fulfilling prophecy. As the Persian poet, Hafiz, quoted "the words you speak become the house you live in." Instead of tearing down the walls, we need to build a healthy home and environment to surround ourselves and protect us from these fears!

FEAR IS UNHEALTHY

We started off with an explanation for this whole fight-or-flight response in times of danger or stress. In the ancient world—and even up to recent times in some parts of the world—those were valid responses to living in dangerous times. In times of war, the fight or flight kicked in to save your life. If you found yourself lost in the woods, the response might also save your life. In today's world, the dangers come less from monsters in the woods and more from corporate relations, personal relationships, or even while sitting in traffic. The problem is, there truly is no one to fight, and running away isn't an option when you're stuck in a cubicle or trapped in traffic on the expressway.

"In our stressed-out world, the fight-or-flight response that kept our ancestors alive has turned into a 'stew and chew,'" according to Pamela Peeke, an assistant clinical professor of medicine at the University of Maryland. If you're ready for a big confrontation but there ends up being no action, the high levels of stress hormones have a physical effect on the body. They stimulate the appetite, which in turn stimulates the growth of fat cells.

The brain is programmed to keep you hiding under a rock so the big, bad monsters will keep walking around you. Therefore, it is no longer serving its purpose. It was meant to make sure you eat and sleep and run away as fast as you can. That's not a good way to live, and it's counter-intuitive when it comes to growing into a well-adjusted, happy, and healthy human being.

ACTION is a big problem for a lot of people because most of us are afraid to take CONSISTENT

ACTION. Most of us wrap our minds around the need to take action. Unfortunately, we think that we only need to take action one time in a big way, and the rest will follow. It doesn't work that way.

If you've ever worked on a big project, such as getting a college diploma or building a successful business, you likely noticed that it required consistent action. You didn't just get the reward the first time you pressed the lever or swung the bat. You had to keep trying over and over again, despite the fact that there were obstacles in the way. Consistent action trips people up because we are afraid that the road ahead is long and hard. We tend to focus on the obstacles. The more we look at the obstacles, the more we lose sight of our ultimate destination. We get taken aback by the stuff we need to let go.

We need to examine and understand fear, learn about it, and then be able to MOVE THROUGH IT in order to take that next step or leap of faith!

THE POWER OF FACING FEAR

The amygdala is at the core of everything our brains take in. But it can be changed. No, we're not talking about having brain surgery to have it removed. Instead, we're going to look at a process a lot less painful. We need to reprogram the amygdala so that instead of you serving it, the amygdala starts working *for you*. We need to realize is that the amygdala is still a necessary organ. We do legitimately require that fight-or-flight response. It's what keeps us alert when out jogging alone at night. It helps us to jump out of the way if we're about to be hit by a bus. While all of those instant reactions still need to be there, our response to the stimuli potentially needs to change. That will enable us to alter the outcome when we realize that we do not have reason to fear, after all.

In other words, how you react to fear will begin to change the way you experience fear.

You've probably heard over and over again that the only way to conquer fear is to face it. But that doesn't mean living a life without fear, as that would be going too far in the opposite direction. Remember, some fear is necessary; what you need to do is to reprogram your reaction to it. To reach past the fight-or-flight response and instead use fear to get ahead and accomplish what you most desire. Stage actors are trained to use their fear of walking out onto a stage to heighten the energy of the performance. They use that fight or flight adrenaline to vocalize and play the part with more passion and energy than they might have otherwise been able to. Using the fear response in positive ways can help change your life. How? Let's find out.

Fear makes you more agile-minded. As long as you challenge your brain, it will get stronger. As with any muscle, when you give it a chance to grow, it will do just that. Learning increases neuroplasticity, meaning that the brain becomes more agile and neurons fire and connect more efficiently. As a side note, at one time there was a theory that once you reached a certain age, you could not change those neural connections. But this theory turned out to be wrong. No matter your age, it's always possible to learn more, and learning more is what increases the brain's power.

You start with the realization that facing your fears requires a new way of thinking. Begin with the idea that risk is not inherently bad, and change is not dangerous. Those ideas alone might take some time to wrap your head around because they go against a lot of what you were raised to believe. After all, every school child is first taught to do things the way everyone before them has done those very things. The workplace can easily sink into the same mindset. Have you ever been part of an organization that has done things a certain way because "it's the way we've always done it"? Keep in mind that thinking outside the box is what leads to growth. And trying something in a new way is more likely to have a new result than simply doing the same thing over and over again. Remember, just because something is messy or difficult doesn't mean it's bad. Facing fear also involves learning about alternatives.

In the end, it's *good* to try new things. And, believe it or not, the world probably won't explode.

When you do venture out, you're going to want to take time afterward to assess your experience. What *did* happen when you tried things a new way? Was it rough? Maybe. But, in all likelihood, it was also survivable, and maybe something good came from the mess. Being locked in the cage or under the rock to preserve the status quo does not lead to knowledge, and it will never lend itself to growth. Facing fear and moving *through* it, however, does.

USING FEAR TO HELP YOU REACT

You know what it's like to be afraid. You sweat, you can't breathe, your heart races, and blood pounds in your ears. Your muscles tense and shake. These are not pleasant sensations. However, much of the time, giving in to fear is a combination of avoiding risk and trying to get rid of the symptoms of fear itself. Facing fears has a similar physical effect on the body. When you face your fears and succeed at conquering them, your body releases chemicals such as endorphins, oxytocin, dopamine, and serotonin—the "feel good" chemicals. It's the sort of rush that adrenaline junkies get when they're base jumping off a bridge or ziplining at top speed through a forest. What you need to understand is that the "feel good" chemical effect lasts longer and is usually more intense than the ill-feeling effects of the fear. So, not only is facing fears healthy, it can get downright addictive.

USING FEAR TO HELP YOU FOCUS

Performing on a stage is a way to focus on using fear. If you're anxious about something, it's difficult to ignore it. Instead, see if you can use that fear to channel the energy into figuring out why you're apprehensive and doing something positive to redirect it. You have instincts; you have judgment if you will only listen to your feelings. Fear is a feeling. It's telling you that there is something about a specific moment that isn't right or healthy or productive. Look for the reason behind the fear. If you're suffering from anxiety due to an upcoming test, does that perhaps mean you haven't studied enough? If you're anxious about presenting a report during a meeting at work, does that mean that maybe you're not well-prepared? Use fear as a divining rod; let it point out the problems and identify the areas that need work. Just don't let it have the reins.

USING FEAR TO HELP MAKE YOU VULNERABLE

The amygdala was created to keep us from becoming vulnerable. However, vulnerability is the birthplace of creativity and innovation. Dr. Brené Brown, a research professor at the University of Houston and best-selling author, put it this way: "Vulnerability is not weakness. And that myth is profoundly dangerous." She further went on to express how it is from that place of vulnerability that growth occurs. Being vulnerable in the jungle might not be a wise choice, but not being vulnerable to a loved one or a partner will create a chasm between you that may be insurmountable. Too many people have pushed someone away because they were afraid they would be left, only to create that very situation. What's worse, in so doing they may have missed the opportunity to find the one person who wouldn't have left them in the first place.

USING FEAR TO PLAN AHEAD

There are legitimate fears, of course. There is fear of the dark alley, fear of getting fired, fear of falling short. These fears are not to be dismissed but are useful in forming a backup plan. Many companies have an emergency data plan. What would happen if all the servers failed or were hacked or flooded? Because of these real contingencies, data is backed up, saved offsite, and preserved with an emergency restoration plan. If you're afraid of losing your job, make contingencies. Begin saving for an emergency, and look at what requirements you need to meet in order to find another position. If you're afraid of losing a client, create a contingency plan that doesn't require that you rely so heavily on a single customer.

USING FEAR TO CONNECT TO OTHERS

You know how fear *feels*—so say we all. Everyone knows what it's like to be paralyzed with fear—to feel the tremors and shortness of breath and racing heart. Facing fear will connect you with others because it's something you have in common with every person alive. By facing your fears, you might wind up inspiring someone else to do the same. Not to mention, helping others through their fears is a strong motivator toward succeeding in facing fears of your own. When you sympathize and share your own story, you help others see that they are not alone. Fear increases your compassion and your ability to offer consolation. What's more, seeing the people around you facing their fears might, in turn, inspire you.

USING FEAR TO BOUNCE BACK

Facing fear creates resilience. You will rise above the fear. You will become stronger and less controlled by your fears the more you face them. Facing fear makes you tougher and gives you the chance to grow in ways you likely haven't even thought of yet. Some people seem to coast through life, always gracefully riding the wave. Chances are, these people don't have it any easier, they've just gotten more resilient, more used to conquering fear and self-doubt.

Facing your fears not only unblocks the way for you to grow and succeed but it also has health benefits across the spectrum—physical, mental, and emotional. Facing your fears has long-term benefits as well. A person without fear is simply someone who isn't paying attention. We all have it, we all experience it. What you do with it is what makes the difference. Don't let an emotion from the smallest part of your mind rule you. You are more than your amygdala. Why are you being ruled by a tiny piece of your brain? And, while you can't deny fear or pretend it's not there, you can give it its proper place in your life. After all, fear is important - sometimes. But it's just one tiny piece of your emotions.

The 5-Step Fear Conquering System

While fears have their place, what we most need is to find some way to reduce them—or at least filter them through rational thought. Facing fear is the application of exactly that kind of filter to every aspect of our lives. The question is, how do we set about facing our fears?

Well, it certainly doesn't mean grabbing that hot burner on the stove. That's not facing fear, that's being less than smart. But, when you understand *why* the fear is there (in this case, saving you from a third-degree burn) you're better able to handle the effects of being near the stove to cook. So, perhaps, if your fear is being burned while cooking, maybe a powerful way to face that fear would be to take some cooking lessons that would teach you how to use the stove properly, without being burned.

Fear is often irrational and immediate. Your amygdala doesn't have room for specifics. In the forest, it didn't matter if the scary part of that saber-tooth tiger was its immense fangs or its six-inch claws. The size of the *cat itself* was enough to make a person run.

HOW DO WE CONQUER FEAR?

Define the Problem

Fear is an indicator. It's a warning that something is wrong, or potentially wrong. Fear exists to enable you to prepare or alter the course of the coming issue. Facing your fear begins with focusing on what scares you. Start with knowing your fears by taking quiet time to have a good look at the fears that are holding you back. What scares you the most? What worries keep you awake at night? What do you think you'll never be able to achieve?

Are you feeling anxious about visiting relatives? Ask yourself why, and get very specific. Which relative, in particular, makes you anxious? What do you expect to happen? Maybe you're dreading another lecture from your mother-in-law. Or, is it the uncle who's always needing to borrow money? Or, do you dread the criticism from that great aunt who disapproves of the way you dress? What specific detail is holding you back from being excited about that family reunion? Once you understand the reasons for the fear, you can make your plan to resolve the situation before it even begins. You can rehearse what you're going to say to your mother-in-law. You can leave your wallet in the car so that you can honestly tell your uncle that you haven't a dime on you. Or, you can practice that snappy comeback for the fashion-blind great aunt. At the very least, setup a strategy to practice your diplomacy. No matter the case, once you've discovered the thing that's causing the anxiety, you can identify a plan that's going to take it right out of the picture.

Are you afraid of public speaking? If so, you're not alone; it's one of the most common fears. What part of it scares you? The possibility of being laughed at or judged? Not trusting yourself to be articulate? Isolate the specific instance that causes your fear. Then, make a strategy to resolve it. Remember, fear is an indicator that you need to prepare or alter something. Once you assess and know what it is that you're afraid of, you can take action to minimize or altogether avoid that outcome.

Once you've pinned down your fears, you can start to tackle them and take away their power. Mindset plays a huge role in dealing with your fears, as negative self-talk feeds self-doubt and eats away at your power to combat your worries. The human brain is adaptable, and it is not difficult to reprogram your mindset.

Choose to take off the negative glasses that distort your fears into seeming bigger than they are. Replace words like "can't," "impossible," or "never" with strong positive language like "I choose," "I can," and "I deserve." If you can turn your mindset around and focus on the good things in your life, you'll find that you'll become more upbeat, more optimistic. Your confidence will increase, and you'll stop expecting things to go wrong and instead begin expecting things to go your way. That perspective is, after all, a key ingredient of success. As a bonus, you'll find that optimism is infectious. It sets up a positivity loop. You'll be happier, and the people around you will be happier as well.

Acknowledge the Fear

Don't try to ignore fear. The little warning message in your mind is doing something important. It's trying to keep you alive, safe, and secure. That's what it's there for, and that is its only job. Pretending it's not there will only make it worse. The suppressed emotion is the one that takes over. Fear is a basic human instinct. Without it, you would likely take foolish risks. But, too much fear can be just as bad from a risk management point of view. Too much fear can stop you from becoming your best self. Successful people learn to face their fears, assess real threats, and use their energy to get where they want to be. On the other hand, fear can paralyze and confuse you. Once you learn how to take control of your fears, you don't have to feel stuck, as eventually they will shrink down to more appropriate proportions. Don't let fear of the unknown stop you from TAKING ACTION.

Your conscious mind strives for wealth or fame or success, and it would seem that the brain does the exact opposite, but that's not the case. Let your fears be heard and understood. Write them out on a piece of paper so that they can be aired and processed. Understand, this is different from speaking them into existence and letting it affect our beliefs in our own abilities and potential. Sometimes seeing them in black and white helps—a lot. You need to write your fears down with pen and paper; don't use a computer. Studies have shown that the mind retains things better that are written out by hand. Getting your fears on paper can take a lot of the sting out of them. Once they're out of your head and on the page, they have a lot less energy, and you can start to assess them to see how much reality is truly there. Chances are, none of them will stand up to much scrutiny. Writing "What if I screw up my presentation?" on paper immediately gives you somewhere to start. Ask questions; test your hypothesis. Why do you think that? What evidence supports this belief? Your answers will give you clues about how to deal with the fear. If you're worried about your presentation skills, ask a colleague to help you rehearse. Get some public speaking training. Make sure your slides and handouts are robust and free of mistakes.

Acknowledge the fear, but don't let it dictate your reaction. If you allow the fear to be heard and understood, it's less likely to become the mountainous obstacle that it has been in the past. You will improve your chances of success if you take your big goal and break it down into bite-sized pieces. Every little success will build a strong foundation of increased self-confidence and decreased fear.

Each time you start to experience fear, writing down a list of the things you fear or hate doing helps! If making a difficult phone call or replying to an email fills you with dread, assign one scary task to every day of the week. Check off each fear as you go, and feel the weight of dread leave your body. That feeling of achievement and pride can become addictive and set up a positive feedback loop. Soon, the tasks you once dreaded won't feel so bad after all, and you'll check them off your list without thinking twice.

All those bite-sized achievements turn into stepping-stones to success and self-confidence. Find the core reason for the overlying fear, prepare for it as best you can, and thank that part of you for keeping you safe. Sometimes, overcoming fear can be as simple as admitting it.

Make A Plan

A better life is often sought as a key to happiness. That's what the brain wants for you too. In the case of the amygdala, however, "happy" means not taking risks that might make you unhappy. Oddly enough, both parts of your brain have the same ultimate goal when it comes to you: your happiness.

Sometimes we get focused on the map, seeing only the how-to-get-there part and forgetting the destination. When fear strikes, remind yourself out loud that you are seeking to benefit, that your goal is to be happy and healthy. Dealing with fears means TAKING ACTION, and the best way to do that is to have a plan. Treat it as a project and work out your big goals; intermediate goals; and milestones, timelines, and resources.

Sometimes, the best way to disarm your fear is to outsmart it. Work out what your fear is telling you to do. Maybe it's highlighting a weakness or a skill you need to develop. Turn it around and use it to your advantage. Minimize your stage fright by getting some training in public speaking or interview skills. Make sure your preparation is thorough. Do your research, write speaking notes, and do some dry runs. Rehearse with a friend or colleague. No one would expect you to parachute out of a plane without proper preparation; tackle your fears in the same way.

There are all sorts of techniques you can use to overcome your fears. You can keep a journal, meditate, or use visualizations to help identify and neutralize the fears that are holding you back. Some people have small rituals that help them overcome stage fright or interview nerves. Others find that positive quotes or affirmations keep them motivated. There are apps, books, websites, and podcasts full of advice on how to overcome fear and anxiety. Go and try a few to see what works best for you.

Everyone is afraid of something. Fear is a normal human emotion, and you can be certain that all the successful people you admire have had to overcome some fear in their life. Many famous actors have overcome crippling stage fright to pursue the career they love. Writers have to deal with the fear of the blank page or the fear of writing the follow-up to their bestseller. You can bet that the first men in space were afraid. Investigate people you admire—find podcasts or articles or memoirs or TED talks. Find out what they overcame in order to be successful.

Take the emotion out of your fears, and you'll be able to tackle them in an objective and business-like way. They'll stop being so overwhelming and turn out to be just another problem you can solve.

Say It Out Loud

Speaking your fears out loud can be very useful. It lets your mind know that, without a doubt, you heard the fears, acknowledged the concern, and accepted the warnings. Hearing it said out loud is a very powerful way to start to reprogram your response system.

Then, tell that part of you what the real fear is. What happens in five years if there is no growth? What happens in ten or twenty years? Are you worried about whether or not you'll succeed? Should you take risks or not? Do you have another five, ten, or twenty years? How "happy" will you be when you're in the same job, or the same place, you've always been? Let that little brain worry about *not* taking a chance. Let it worry about being too safe, not taking any chances. If you're afraid of dating, make that amygdala focus on what it would be like to be alone for another year.

You can also share your fears with someone as you speak them out loud. No one said you had to overcome your fears all by yourself. It's okay to ask for help. At the very least, you'll likely need informal support from the people who know you best and believe in you. Your family and friends make the best cheer squad. They'll be there for you to help you through the tough times and toast your successes. Tell them what you're trying to do and get their help. It's always a good idea to find a mentor or coach you can trust—someone you can go to for advice or who can connect you to the right people.

And, if you have trouble with anxiety, get professional help. You wouldn't think twice about getting your car fixed, so why struggle through fears when there are lots of professional help options?

Speak it and switch the tables, let your amygdala start working *with* you instead of against you.

Accept the Fear and Move Through It

At times, fear can create depression, anxiety, and more fear. It can be an endless loop that feeds on itself. If your thoughts are on what *isn't happening,* or on what *falls short*, you're feeding into this loop. Fear cannot take root in positive thoughts—expecting the best outcome, being proactive, remembering what you have accomplished up to now. Any or all of these will not allow fear to become overwhelming.

Worry has a way of distorting reality, especially at 4am when you've been lying awake fretting. The first thing to do in order to shrink your fears back down to a manageable size is to try to assess how likely it is that your fear will come true. On a scale of one to ten, how likely is it that you'll go broke or never get promoted? Second, what's the worst that can happen if one of the feared realities does come to pass? You might have to tighten your budget or stay in your current job a while longer. Third, look back on your previous experience. You are certain to have more successes than failures in your life. You've made it this far, after all.

Fears Can Act as Powerful Filters and Provide Insight Into Your Power

They blind you to what you've already achieved. If you're feeling pessimistic about your chances of success, step back for a minute and count up all the successes you already have under your belt. What mountains have you already climbed? Think of the promotions you've already earned, and the job interviews you've rocked. Remember graduating or passing your driving test. All those successes, big and small, brought you to where you are today. Don't let fear downgrade that effort.

Facing fear is about reprograming the oldest and most basic part of the mind. What you do every day in every waking moment programs the rest of your mind. If you continually tell yourself that you're incapable, you become incapable. If you constantly tell yourself you're afraid, the fear will never leave you. Replacing fear with positive thoughts will not only reprogram the amygdala but it will also reprogram *you*. You exactly are who you think you are. "What you believe, you achieve" as the saying goes, even if what you believe is dark and fearful. There are many ways to face fear, but the surest way to *confront* your fear is through logic and reason. The amygdala doesn't reason, but reason confounds fear. Analyze, scrutinize, and classify your fears. Acknowledge them, thank them for the warning, and continue on.

Also, be easy on yourself. All of this will take considerable practice, but it will work in the end. If you're consistent you're going to see some positive and exciting change in a fairly short time.

We are now much more confident moving THROUGH fear. We refuse to let it stop us from doing things. We have learned time and time again that each step forward consistently shows us that there are so many things waiting just on the other side of fear, but we can't skirt around it. We can't avoid it. You have to move *through* it!

Moving through fear means that you have to continue to move forward no matter what. If you are scared, do it anyway. The hardest part is taking that first step. It's like jumping into water when you know it may be cold. Some of us creep in, allowing our body temperature to slowly adjust. Some dip that toe in first and then jump ALL IN. We are not here to argue that one way is better than the other, because the point is…you are still moving forward regardless. The biggest fear many of us face is the fear of failure, but how will you ever truly know that you will fail if you don't even try?

It's TIME to Take Your POWER BACK!

Your fears are not autonomous entities. Often, they turn out to be merely creations of your imagination. Sure, you may have learned some in childhood, but they are still your fears. They are in your head, and you are the only one who can kick them out. A lot of your fears might well turn out to be like the Wizard of Oz—a little bald guy with a megaphone, hiding behind a curtain. A fraudster. And you have both the power and the responsibility to be an adult and kick them out! How dare they try to poison your ambition, try to stop you from being your best you? You're bigger and smarter than your fears. Take your power back and get mad at them. Who are they to take over your life and stop you from being confident and happy? Give them the boot, and reclaim your mental space.

In the science fiction classic, *Dune*, Frank Herbert wrote:

"Fear is the mind-killer. Fear is the little-death that brings total obliteration. I will face my fear. I will permit it to pass over me and through me."

The term "mind-killer" is spot-on. Fear removes logic and reason. Fear overrides our higher thought processes and reduces us to a lower level. Living in fear means restricting your life. Remember that the amygdala wants to keep you safe at any cost. If that means staying under a rock, so be it. Only by being able to face our fears through acknowledging them are we able to set them aside. Let these things "pass over and through," as Herbert penned, so that we might reach the other side of fear where it no longer can control us.

Relegate fear to its intended use: a warning system. That relegates fear to the role of something not to be ignored, something that is instead an indication of something you need to deal with—maybe not in the fight-or-flight way, but in another manner altogether. Remember, fear does not have to mean the end of everything. Instead, allow fear to be useful, especially when it provides the energy we need to funnel into that pitch, or as the enthusiasm we need to make that speech, or even the extra burst of speed we need to catch that bus.

UNDERSTAND THE WARNING SIGNS

Tapping into fear is a way to harness your energy differently. But first, we need to understand the warning signs so that we might ultimately free ourselves from its crippling effects. Becoming buried under fear is a weakness, but tapping into it is a strength. Take notice the next time you're afraid. Do you shake? Jump up and down? Feel like you need to suddenly fly off in many different directions? That's the adrenaline pumping. Congratulations, you have just been given a burst of energy to handle the upcoming event, to prepare for what *might* go wrong. Use that to realize that, should an issue arrive, you're prepared to circumvent it, and then use the burst of energy you've been given to handle it.

Are you unable to "do" something to prevent whatever scares you? Focus on controlling the controllable. Get some perspective, and realize that most of your fears don't involve life-threatening situations. Public-speaking, job interviews, exams, or family functions—even sorting out your debts—might feel uncomfortable, but they're all achievable challenges. Take back control by assessing what you can change and what you can't, and letting go of the things you can't control. Worrying over things outside of your control is a waste of energy. Perhaps there's nothing to be done? Go and get some exercise, do something physically active. If you can ride it out and let the adrenaline run through your system, there are endorphins in your future. Since everything goes through the amygdala, the more you train it to accept logic and optimism, the more you will be able to reprogram it to behave as an essential part of your personal growth, and fewer things will stand in your way.

Once you have made the decision to move forward, we have found that what tends to squash our fear over and over again is consistent ACTION combined with an accountability partner. Each time we are faced with fear, good accountability partners have been able to help move through the fear by challenging each other to take action. Action can include coming up with solutions to whittle away the unknown and the fear that comes with it. Action can include pushing through the fear with encouragement and confidence, offering alternatives to conquer the fearful situation, or allowing practice to release the fear by developing expertise.

Conquering fear over and over is something we will have to learn and TAKING CONSISTENT ACTION will lead to this!

Retraining your brain is possible. Be patient and kind to yourself. Remember that you've made it this far, and that there's no telling how much further you can go by leading your fears and not being led by them. Can you recall the last time you felt afraid of something and did it anyway? It is time to TAKE the FIRST STEP of ACTION, move through fear, and Do. It. Scared.

Chapter Review

- People who succeed are people who take risks.
- Some fear is necessary, and what you need to do is to reprogram your reaction to it.
- Facing fear also means learning about alternatives.
- Fear exists to enable you to prepare or alter the oncoming issue.
- Challenge: Each time you start to experience fear, write down a list of things you fear or dislike. Assign one scary task to every day of the week and start checking items off the list.
- Replacing fear with positive thoughts will not only reprogram the amygdala but it will also reprogram *you*.

Time to ACT!

Today's Date:

Assess – Journal about what you wish to take action on related to this chapter's topic.

Commit – Write down the action you are willing to commit to in the next twelve months.

Transform – Identify an actionable goal that will transform the commitment into a measurable outcome.

CHAPTER THREE

REMOVE YOUR BLINDERS (SELF-WORTH/VALUE)

"She remembered who she was and the game changed."
—Lalah Delia

Do you believe in your own potential?

While we all have our own dreams and aspirations, few of us are fully aware of and have belief in our own potential. It can be hard to see the good and admirable traits in ourselves, just as it can be hard to see our faults.

NATALIE'S STORY

I struggled to see my self-worth and value for

years. This manifested in a few ways:

As an audiologist, I worked hard to learn everything I could because, one, I was truly interested in learning everything I could, and two, I wanted to make myself as marketable and indispensable as possible. Along the way, I didn't like knowing I was also in "sales," and often did not like to refer to myself as a salesperson. Alternately, I'd tell myself that I didn't learn how to sell in school and in my training, and I was therefore terrible at it. This bled into not knowing or feeling comfortable with how much to ask for when it came down to what I wanted to make as a "salary." I never understood how people decide who makes what in a certain profession or industry. So much so that I began to question, "Just how much do I ask for?"

I had a chance to remedy this as I sat down with a savvy businessman one evening and asked him to show me how to justify my requested salary or profit share and teach me how to negotiate. This soon grew my confidence and became a skill that I could teach others as well as use in other areas in my life any time I had to negotiate—buying a home, purchasing a car, general business transactions. I never backed down, and my confidence and preparation allowed me to continue to push to acquire positive outcomes. However, with one hurdle came yet another. Once I could negotiate, I dealt with the fact that I didn't own my own audiology practice and therefore worked with an ear, nose, and throat physician. Even though it is much different from a typical set-up due to my negotiations and experience as well as the fact that it is the best scenario for my family and me; and although I am independent and autonomous and work with a very fair and understanding physician who owns the practice, comments and bias from colleagues about my working with a physician who owns the practice did not stop. Neither did my struggle to see my self-worth. It helped that I knew the agreement, but jabs from the outside continued to feel like that pebble in my shoe that I couldn't get rid of.

While working as an audiologist, I began my foray into a new environment—my charter into the unknown—during which I observed and worked in an entrepreneurial and start-up business space for a few years. Each time the question "What are you working on?" or "What do you do?" or "What do you need help with?" was asked, I was scared to answer. Partly because I didn't know the answer. I didn't believe in my capabilities and that I could start a business outside of Audiology. Once I *did* know what I could do, what I had fun doing, how happy it made me, and how I was able to help others easily, I still feared that there was no way I could accomplish my goal because I didn't know where to start and/or didn't have the right training, studies, certification, or degree. Once that was no longer an issue, I was willing to try working toward the goal, but I don't think it would work.

This was followed by "I know and see that I am good at this, but I still don't truly believe in my ability." In addition, how could I possibly expect someone to pay me to show them how to do something that I did not "go to school" for, and how much would I even ask them to pay me? Why do we do this to ourselves?

One of the most crucial steps in developing your self-confidence and achieving all that you are capable of starts with believing in your own potential. Once you start believing in yourself and all that you can be, it can help you look at new opportunities, try new things, challenge yourself, and take risks that you may not have felt comfortable taking before, all leading to further success. Are you unsure of whether or not you believe in your potential? If so, here are some ways to help:

Spend Time in Self-Reflection

Spending time in self-reflection allows you to ask yourself what you are capable of and reflect on your strengths and admirable qualities, and it then provides time for you to pause to provide thoughtful answers. Time spent determining your potential is truly valuable to both who you are as a person and to being able to achieve that full potential. During this time, try to also focus on the following questions:
- What is my true potential?
- What do I want to achieve?

- Do I believe I can achieve it?
- What action can I take, and what can I do with this potential?

Focusing and answering these questions helps you identify your potential and you will be able to believe in it more rapidly and strongly.

Write Down What You See as Your Potential
Once you have taken the time to reflect on your potential, writing down and listing qualities and skills makes them more real and keeps you accountable to your beliefs. The next step is to study this list and keep it with you to ensure that you can look at it whenever you feel yourself doubting your potential. Carry it with you in your wallet. Post it on your mirror to look at while you are getting ready in the morning. Keeping your potential in the forefront of your mind will help you truly believe in it.

Prove Your Potential to Yourself
For some people, in order to truly believe in something, they need to be able to see it. This can extend to what they believe about themselves. How can you prove to yourself that you have potential? Simple: you ACT on it! Start by challenging yourself to push the limits of your potential. These challenges can be in your career, your relationships, or your hobbies; as long as it challenges you, it will force you to show-

case your full potential. Once you have achieved the goal you set for yourself, you will have a well-earned sense of accomplishment and a newfound confidence, and you will start to fully believe in your potential without doubts.

UNDERSTANDING YOUR CORE VALUES

We believe that understanding who you are and how to value yourself begins with understanding what you value as your life's priorities. These priorities are your core values. Once you are able to define these critical values, you can confidently exist with them as your guideposts in life. They will help you to make decisions swiftly and with confidence, they will ensure that you are using your time and energy wisely, they will allow you to align your actions with your priorities, and they will aid in improving your relationships with others. We look at them as a filtration system. Every decision that you are confronted with for your life should be measured against your core values to determine if they are in alignment. This allows you to filter out those things that do not support your priorities and are out of alignment.

Defining your core involves sitting down in a quiet space and examining what is most important to you. You must ask yourself some important questions about your life and what you wish to see as outcomes for your life. Consider your family, relationships, life's dreams, desires, and your natural behaviors and attitudes. These all play a vital role in defining your core values. Once you have defined your core values, place them somewhere that you will see them daily. Do this until you are able to memorize them and easily recall what they are. Also, be aware that core values can change over time. This is due to changing circumstances, experiences, and overall maturity through life. It is a good idea to review your core values annually and do not be afraid to change them or reprioritize them if needed. We have included access to our core values training and worksheets in the ACT Now Resource Library that is available to those who purchase this book. See the Appendix for instructions on accessing this valuable resource.

DOES INNATE SELF-WORTH EXIST?

Throughout our lives, we are subjected to ups and down as well as good and bad times. Each of these external experiences helps to develop our self-esteem. Self-worth, on the other hand, occurs internally, without the need for any external validation. Many people use the terms self-esteem and self-worth interchangeably, but self-esteem relies on external factors, while self-worth relies on internal thinking.

Self-worth is not dependent upon things that you are good at, how smart or beautiful you are, or what you have accomplished throughout your life. These are all external factors that increase your self-esteem. Again, self-worth is innate—it comes from within and is based on the strength of your belief that you deserve what you desire as well as that you are inherently "good enough" to have it.

Another way to think of it is, if you fail at something, the failure itself is bound to affect your self-esteem. This feeling may last for a short while. On the other hand, failing at something will *not* affect your self-worth, because you already know that failure and success are simply two sides of the same coin, both of which you need in your experiences in order to become a well-rounded person. Your self-worth doesn't change; you know that you *are* worthy, no matter what. When you have a solid understanding that you are born a worthy individual, that understanding becomes a part of you. People are able to strengthen that sense of worthiness by taking actions that reinforce their self-worth beliefs. There are many of ways to grow and maintain your self-worth, such as taking proper care of yourself, being kind to yourself, getting exercise when you need it, saying no when something doesn't feel right, and making sure that you have what you need.

WAYS TO TAP INTO YOUR SELF-WORTH
Know and Understand Yourself

People may think they know who they are, but it's important to be clear that knowing who you are has nothing to do with the things you own, the car you drive, the clothes you wear, or how much money you make. It isn't about your education, your degree (or lack thereof), or whether or not you are in a meaningful relationship. Understanding yourself is really about knowing what makes you uniquely you. What do you like or love; what do dislike? What do you enjoy doing? What types of things and ways of experiencing those things do you value? A great question start with is, "What do I value about myself?" If everything you own and love were to be taken from you tomorrow and all you had left was yourself, what would you be able to do and offer the world?

Accept Yourself as You Are

Accepting yourself starts by valuing who you are in this present moment. The good news is that who you are in the present moment does not take into account things you may have done in the past. Being able to accept yourself means that you do not spend time in judgement—looking back, or even looking forward. You are just in the here and now, in the *what* of who you are at this moment—the good and bad, the perfect and flawed parts of yourself.

Unconditionally Love Yourself

Learning to love and care for yourself is a large part of increasing your self-worth. This can be accomplished through the practice of positive and compassionate thinking, both about yourself and *to* yourself. Let go of self-loathing, negative self-talk and any negative thinking patterns. Everyone has flaws and faults. Although we tend to see them more easily and quickly in ourselves, they do not negate our value, but instead help make up who we are as individuals.

Recognize Yourself

Self-worth is truly understanding and realizing that external things—including people, places, and circumstances—have no bearing on who you are and what you are worth. It becomes easier to let go of these external factors, as they do not serve you and are not part of your identity. The growth of a stronger sense of self no longer relies on them.

Take Full Responsibility

Taking responsibility for your thoughts leads you to acknowledge that you are in control. You are always the only one responsible for your problems, unique life experiences, and circumstances. You have the power to control your world.

Innate self-worth gives you the ability to accept and celebrate yourself along with the uniqueness that makes you different from everyone else. You understand that no matter what you look like, how much you weigh, or how much money you have in the bank, you are worthy of love and being loved...simply because you are you. If you feel your self-worth fading, spend time around those who love you unconditionally, as that provides a constant reminder of your own innate worth. Do the things you know you are talented at doing. Go back in your mind and relive past successes and celebrations, reminding yourself that you are worthy, and nothing external can change that.

NATALIE'S STORY

What slowly began to change was, I began to start to listen more. I had all these amazing people around me not only doing things for themselves and believing in themselves but also checking in with and encouraging me. I continued to retort, "But...I'm JUST a (fill in the blank)." What my friendship with Regeanie taught me was that I needed to take off the blinders. I needed to understand that it isn't all about me. Not that I ever truly believed that it was, but *not* walking in my purpose and fulfilling what I was created to do caused me to live in a hole, unable to help someone who may have been waiting for me to accept who I was and fully arrive.

I would still often say, "I don't see how I help and motivate people; I am just being me!" Regeanie replied, "It's all God and how HE puts people in our lives who we need. Sometimes it is for a season, and sometimes people are with us until our life ends. What is way cool is when He puts people together who are able to have bi-directional value and benefit to each other."

Surround Yourself with the RIGHT People Who Believe in Your Potential

This is one of the most important actions in which we believe, and one of the essential reasons we decided to write this book! It would be nice to think that we don't ever let others' words or actions affect us, but the truth is that the people we have around us, especially those who may be closest to us, do indeed have a profound effect on us and our emotions. If the people closest to you show that they doubt your potential, you're likely to do the same because you trust them and believe that they may see you in the highest light. *But*, it is important to understand that words even from people who love and care for you can still have a negative influence in your life. When you surround yourself with people who believe in your potential, it starts to feel like encouragement to help you achieve all you can. The positive influence of their words will provide you with the elevation you need to help you further see and believe in your potential. It is time to take *off* the blinders. It is time to stop having tunnel vision and be open to the fact that what you do matters. Even if you don't yet see it, others do!

Part of owning your self-worth and knowing your value is, one, investing in yourself and, two, being comfortable and confident enough to get paid for what you are doing. We aren't sure whether one is easier than the other, but let's start with what we do know. We know that investing in yourself is necessary. Investing in yourself includes asking for and accepting help based on the fact that you know you want to improve. Investing in yourself to learn something new can be downright exciting. Learning from others allows you to open yourself up to so many new ideas and connections. Further, it starts the process of you paying someone else for what *they* are worth. Do you see where this is leading? If you are able to pay someone else for what they are worth, why wouldn't you charge for providing something that you can uniquely provide or teach?

NATALIE'S STORY

Regeanie suggested that I start being paid for all the help I was providing other people with social media. I thought that what came easily to me should come easily to others. Or, that I just "do what I do"—how could I possibly get paid for doing it?! She assured me that what I do is *not* easy for others, and what I believed was a skill I "just got" was definitely something others needed help with.

In addition to this, my self-worth was based on untruths that I was telling myself. I knew of "social media gurus" who claimed themselves as such, which meant that what I did or was able to see in terms of the way individuals and businesses could improve in their social media skills could not possibly be helpful, since I was not known as a "social media guru." I also believed that if I did in fact come out with this new aspect of my business, I would be "taken down" or "blasted" by these other social media gurus.

Regeanie wasn't having any part of that belief system. Even when I tried to argue that I did not have any degree or certification, she shared with me more about her background and where she is now and challenged me by asking whether it would make me feel better to have a certificate or a course. If so, she challenged me to get it done!

Why is Self-Worth So Important?

Believing in our self-worth is one of the greatest gifts we can give ourselves and other human beings. Without a clear appreciation of and belief in our own worth, we simply cannot move forward and impact others' lives in a way that will be beneficial to them. Trying to move ahead without this awareness leads to confused decisions and inauthenticity. Understanding self-worth is also critical in avoiding dangerous and toxic relationships. Having ineffective clarity of your needs versus another's needs may lead you to settle for less than you truly deserve. It seems easy for us to see others' worth, but our view of our own selves can be somewhat difficult to nail down. We are often concerned with what other people think of us, which gets in the way of being able to truly know and love ourselves. We often live our lives based on the acceptance of others, which causes us to have a false sense of our own identity and worth.

Although rewarding, it is not always easy to both achieve a high level of self-worth and maintain it. Self-worth can be learned, therefore do not worry if you grew up with less-than-optimal parenting that may have left you lacking in it. It requires daily effort to identify and further reduce what may come easy for some of us—negative thinking and negative self-talk—and instead can focus on turning those statements into their positive counterparts.

Self-worth is especially important to focus on when in a romantic relationship. If you start off a relationship without valuing yourself, it can be detrimental in many ways. For one, you will almost always settle for less than you deserve in a partner, mostly due to the fact that you just can't imagine meeting your "dream" partner and falling in love with him or her—or even worse, you believe that he or she would never fall in love with you. This can eventually lead you down a road that is unhealthy emotionally and psychologically, and could even end up being dangerous for your safety—especially if you were to meet and fall in love with someone who is toxic.

Self-worth is also important to focus on professionally—between peers as well as between employers and employees. A healthy work environment is one wherein there is mutual respect and an ability to accept positions within the business or company without blurred personal lines of friendship. Toxic business relationships feed into those who are not fully aware of their self-worth. Bullying and intimidation tactics are dangerous and can be costly to reputations and business decisions alike.

A lack of self-worth can lead to a lack of caring for yourself. When you feel that you are not worthy, you tend to focus on others instead of yourself, and then your own needs are not met because you don't feel that they are important. Over time, these decisions and views can lead to further and more extreme problems, especially if you are prone to experiencing depression and anxiety. Negative thoughts along with a lack of self-worth can trigger a downward spiral that can be difficult to recover from once it begins.

Instead, try striving for healthy self-worth levels that keep you cared for, protected, loved, and fulfilled from smaller, sometimes inevitable bumps in the road that might bring you down. If your self-worth is intact and healthy, it mitigates many small failures that can occur in, for example, a business plan or a home project. These tend to be easier to overcome and see as not being big failures after all.

Is There a Difference Between Self-Worth and Self-Esteem?

Many people use the terms self-worth and self-esteem interchangeably, but there are people who believe that these terms are separate and unique concepts.

Let's examine self-worth. How "worthy" do you believe you are? Do you believe you are valued? Do you feel you deserve the things you want and desire? The answer to these questions starts to determine your self-worth. It might come as a surprise, but there are many gifted, talented, and successful individuals who have very low levels of self-worth and continue to subconsciously self-sabotage any potential success at the first opportunity. Sometimes, the larger and more life-changing the potential success in front of them, the harder it is to stop the will to self-sabotage. Self-worth is largely built up during the early childhood years. It begins with your parents as you are essentially told what your own worth is by how they act and react to you along with the quality of attention you get from them. However, the good news is that even if you had a challenging childhood and did not have parents who spoke positive self-worth into you, self-worth is still something that you can work on and build up on your own.

Self-esteem, on the other hand, is dependent on things outside of yourself, sometimes even out of your control. For example, even a small rejection can feel very large and painful, which in turn can immediately change the way we think and feel about ourselves. Even if you do take a hit to your self-esteem, the good news is you can recover quickly by being able to recognize that there are particular and unique things that you do well. The hit to your self-esteem will hurt less and less until it subsides altogether, and you are back to feeling great again!

Self-esteem and self-worth are important facets of a healthy identity. The work it takes to develop and maintain them will pay off towards accomplishing the goal of maintaining a positive outlook.

STEPS TO TAKE WHEN SELF-WORTH IS LOW

Everyone has a time when then have lower-than-normal self-esteem and/or self-worth. It isn't always what happens to us, but how we react that says a lot about who we are. It is important to be very careful, especially during times when your self-worth is low for an extended period of time. Long periods of low self-worth can take a toll both mentally and emotionally and even result in depression. Therefore, it is important to be aware and have resources available with regard to what you can do to mitigate this challenge.

A healthy sense of worthiness can give you a boost, especially when things may look bleak or a failure occurs. The awareness of knowing that something may have simply happened versus believing something to be a failure is based on having an aversion to self-blame along with a healthy sense of self-worth. The ability to see that something happened and extract the lessons from it to reduce replicability is also healthy and helpful in moving ahead. On the other hand, low self-worth often causes one to spend unnecessary and wasted time feeling guilty and blaming oneself, and ultimately may result in the inability to get back on track.

Start to foster healthy self-worth begins with being honest with yourself and the negative people, environments, and things you may have surrounding you in your life. This also includes the negativity that may come from within yourself. Negative thoughts are fairly easy to spot once you are open to realize you're having them. The key is to attempt to turn each negative thought around in order to focus on a positive angle related to the particular situation. In turn, over time you will notice that when negative thoughts arise, you will be better able to prevent them before they take hold by reframing them and thereby retraining your brain to eliminate the negativity.

NATALIE'S STORY

I had solid experience (quite by accident) in the area of reprogramming my mind around the practice of eliminating negativity and instead filling that area with positivity. I was able to use my social media skills paired with my inherent decision not to spread negativity on such an open platform for many to see and possibly be affected by. I struggled—big time. One of the people I had previously thought to be a trusted confidante and friend tore me down behind closed doors, where no one else could see, and her violent and mean persona was entirely different than what she wanted people to perceive her as—someone who was in tune with the earth and grounded in her emotions. I let myself believe her words—that I was truly a nobody who did not own my own practice, that I did not make as much money as she did, and that no one cared about me. To add injury to insult, she did this multiple times, and did not show this part of herself to anyone else. In turn, I lost my connection to many colleagues and acquaintances during this time. I suffered a lot, feeding myself internal self-doubt and low self-worth due to both the words and actions of this person and, in turn, allowing myself to react emotionally by "going dark." But, while I had disappeared from the limelight, I used social media in the exact opposite way to the way I was feeling.

Through my internal struggles of seeing this person keep the status quo and even rise occasionally through false pretenses, with every thought I had that started to root in negativity, I challenged myself to post something that was the complete opposite of my feeling at the time, which meant that it had to be positive and inspiring. I learned many things about myself and my self-worth during this time. I learned that, through it all, no matter how much negativity I was channeling through the hurt, the focus and truth on spreading positivity held true, as it was a core belief and value of mine. I also learned that during a time when I did not believe in my self-worth, I let my own negative feelings and surroundings dictate my thoughts and beliefs. Over time, through the people I surrounded myself with and my reprogramming, I came to find out that these thoughts and beliefs were not true, and it became easier to walk away from the negativity.

One of the best things you can do to help elevate your self-worth when it feels low is to engage in the things you are already great at doing! In addition, you can boost your competence and confidence by diving in and practicing what you already know how to do well.

Don't forget to regularly practice self-compassion along with self-love. Take time to partake in things you find pleasure in and truly enjoy. This could be curling up with a good book; taking a long, hot bath with a glass of wine; or going for a walk. Do things that you may have put off because you've been too busy. Try spending a full hour with no distractions while playing with your kids. Whatever it is, believe that you deserve it, and go do it!

Spend time with the positive people in your life. Everyone should have an inner circle, but on occasion review who is in your circle, as it may be time to revamp your "circle of influence." If you find yourself spending more time with people who bring negativity into your life, it is important to make the conscious decision to evaluate your choices and bring more positive people into your life. You are worth it!

Learn to be your own champion, and assert yourself in positive ways. If you find yourself saying yes out of a sense of guilt or obligation, take time to examine that more closely. Learning to say no gets easier the more you do it, and is arguably one of the most liberating steps you can take!

5 Tips to Maintaining Self-Worth

One of the smartest and healthiest things you can do for yourself is maintain your own self-worth. This is especially true after you may have spent a lot of time learning and building it up within yourself. When you are able to find ways to increase and maintain self-worth, the next step is to repeat these practices in order to set up new and healthy positive habits. Here are some simple and effective ways to help maintain your sense of self-worth.

Appreciate Everything
In order to do this, you have to look up more often

from what you may be working on. Even during the worst of times, it is likely that you still have a lot to be thankful for. There are things that you can appreciate, such as a loving family, a warm home, caring friends, and in most cases, employment. You have food to eat, most of your bills are paid, and you have things you can celebrate and be grateful for. Take the time to practice gratitude every day—even several times a day.

Say NO to Negativity

Make it a goal to remove your own negative self-talk as well as negative people and environments from your life. Tell them all to be quiet. Walk away. Stop being judgmental of others. Remove toxic people from your life, and remove yourself from toxic environments. Instead, bring in more positive. This step alone will do wonders for your self-worth. Many of the things and stories we've told ourselves for years may not be as real or true as we've come to believe. Be sure to keep a reality check in order.

Be Confident of Your Identity

Try not to compare yourself and your life to what you observe in others. Instead, focus on what *you* value and open your eyes to see that you have what you want and can continue striving to attain even more experiences that add to your value. Being confident helps you own your voice to stand up to people when they try to tell you who they think you should be or what they believe your goals should be.

Do Your Best at Everything, Every Time

You never know if you will have a second chance. Accepting only this one fact will keep you working hard to deliver your very best. When you try your hardest, the result is always feeling that you have accomplished something. This in turn feeds your strong sense of self-worth. In anything you do, there is a lot of satisfaction in doing a job well done. Always strive to perform at your highest level. If you do, you will never fall back on any doubt that you are good enough!

Create Relationships with Positive People

This may seem like easy advice, but sometimes positive people can turn into negative people. Always have your awareness intact enough to shift if things change. Positive people do not talk badly about others, nor do they feed on judgement or jealousy. Positive people are givers, and have good intentions behind their giving. They do not give simply to get ahead. Do not continually allow negative people or negative attitudes into your inner circle. Constantly aim to create new relationships with positive people so that you're surrounded by people who will understand you and support you at every level.

NATALIE'S STORY

I have always been thankful for the people and opportunities around me. I am in awe of the technology at our fingertips that allows us to connect to people with whom we never thought we would be able to connect. One of the biggest moments in my life—one that I will never forget—was the day I stepped up to the plate and owned my worth.

As a global ambassador for a women's entrepreneurial group, I was to emcee a global summit filled with entrepreneurs, business owners, and speakers from around the world. Two weeks prior to the summit, I noticed that Dr. Jen Welter, athlete and the first female coach in the NFL, was speaking in the same city on the same weekend. I heard her inspirational talk from stage when I attended the United Nations Foundation Girl Up Summit as an advisor about a year and a half prior. I did not meet her at that particular gathering, but since then, followed her on social media and continued to be motivated and inspired by her message: "Greatness is a choice you make over and over. And when you choose personal greatness—big or small—it becomes a part of who you are…I have had my days when I would not have chosen greatness on my own. It took work. It took strategy. It took perseverance. Don't leave your greatness to chance."

Jen's story of persevering in a man's world continued to draw me in. I wanted to support her and listen to her speak, especially during the time of her own launch of *Play Big: Lessons in Being Limitless From the First Woman to Coach in the NFL*. Because she followed me on Twitter, I ended up tweeting about our summit, tagged her, and let her know I would try my best to support her and listen to her speak in person again.

Almost immediately, I had an idea to have her come speak at our global summit. Due to the time crunch, I was told that if I wanted to include her, I would have to make it happen by reaching out to her myself. Not knowing where to start or what to say, I remember taking a deep breath before taking the *one action step* that helped change my belief in who I am. I sent a direct message through Twitter and described our global summit, offered her a 30-minute spot on stage, and let her know we would be arranging a meet-and-greet and book signing during the summit. I waited. An hour later she responded and agreed, and I took it upon myself to arrange logistics for her to be on stage and have not one, but *two* opportunities to sign her books at our summit—and to think that ONE ACTION made it happen!

After the summit, Jen reached out to talk to me more as a friend. She wondered what I was all about and what I enjoyed doing. She did not want to know about Audiology. She wanted to know about me as a *person*. What happened afterwards was a series of connections and support of each other that led me to bring the first Grrridiron Girls Flag Football camp to Loveland, Colorado with coordinated media appearances for her. Not bad for "just an audiologist!"

We all have a constant flow of potential inside us, but not many people recognize and believe in that potential. Believing in your own self is an essential part of your confidence, journey, and success. If you believe you are capable, you are far more likely to accomplish a goal. It is, however, understandable that believing in your own potential may not come as easily for you as it seems to for others. It helps that, when you do not believe in yourself, you have the right people around you who can see your potential and help you take the next steps. It takes time, and it takes practice. This is an area we often must work on over and over before we prove to ourselves that we believe it. We hope we've helped you to see and believe in your potential.

Chapter Review

- Believing in your own potential is crucial in developing your self-confidence.
- Knowing yourself and your life's priorities or core values is critical to valuing yourself.

- Belief in your potential starts with having to prove it to yourself, act on it, and challenge yourself by pushing the limits.
- Self-worth and self-esteem are NOT the same. Self-worth is based on internal thinking, while self-esteem relies on external factors.
- Without clear understanding and appreciation of your own worth, you will not be able to move forward and impact others' lives in a way that will be beneficial to them.
- Healthy self-worth includes being honest with yourself about the negativity you have surrounding you, especially that which comes from *within* you.

Time to ACT!

Today's Date:

Assess – Journal about what you wish to take action on related to this chapter's topic.

Commit – Write down the action you are willing to commit to in the next twelve months.

Transform – Identify an actionable goal that will transform the commitment into a measurable outcome.

CHAPTER FOUR

THE AHA MOMENTS (EPIPHANIES)

"There's nothing better [than] when something comes and hits you and you think 'YES!'"
—J.K. Rowling

Have you ever experienced a moment in which you suddenly had the greatest clarity about something? Many refer to it as an aha moment. It's as though a bright light is suddenly turned on to illuminate a dark room, and the moment the light comes on, you can see everything for what it truly is. Merriam-Webster defines it as "a usually sudden manifestation or perception of the essential nature or meaning of something."

Media mogul and first female black billionaire, Oprah Winfrey, refers to an aha moment as a moment of sudden insight into yourself—one that draws upon something that you already knew or understood about yourself but did not have clarity on until the aha moment occurred. When you experience that moment, you suddenly have a revelation about or insight into a topic in a way that you never have before, and when that happens, it can come like a startling slap in the face that turns your world upside down.

REGEANIE'S STORY

In 2011, I woke up one morning fully expecting to have a day like any other, as I prepared my children for school and myself for work. I had no idea what I was really in for and how truly different this day would be. It would become a day of transformation, after which my life would never be the same. This was the day when I had an epiphany about my life and career as well as what I had been settling for up until that point.

I was a senior manager responsible for a multimillion-dollar budget and thirty-three employees. My area of responsibility in Cyber Security impacted an internal customer base of more than 100,000 employees, and externally, more than three million end-users. I had an annual six-figure salary, was knowledgeable in my field of work, and enjoyed working with most of the people around me. However, on this particular day in 2011, I arrived at my office, and things literally began to fall apart in front of me. In the first three hours of the day, we experienced multiple security incidents that had negative impact on our network, and I was being pressured to give quick explanations while having staff scurry around to pinpoint the source of the issues. As multiple people entered my office, including the leaders I reported to, answers were demanded. I remember standing at the whiteboard in my office, mapping out the strategy to isolate the issues and pinpoint the root cause of each, and thinking, "This is absolute nuts and stressful! I would love to be somewhere else right now. I can't continue to do this."

Now, let me put the magnitude of this thought into perspective. This was not the first time that I had been involved in a security incident. Actually, I had participated in and led us through many of these incidents over the course of my career. And, if I'm truthful, I have to say that I had always enjoyed them. I loved the adrenaline rush, the problem solving under pressure, and the excitement of it all. You could say that I thrived in the high-stress moments. However, on this day, I didn't enjoy it, I didn't thrive in it; all I wanted to do was walk away from it. I actually felt numb to it. No excitement, just a feeling of emptiness.

As we always did, my team and I handled the problem, and things went back to normal after forty-eight hours of little sleep and high-pressure moments. However, the entire time I couldn't shake that feeling of emptiness. Later that week as I sat quietly in my office writing an incident report, I heard a small voice inside say, "It's time to leave. If you stay, you will become ill and will never live the purpose you were created for." It was in that moment that I knew my career in Information Technology and Cyber Security would soon be ending. It was such a strong feeling, and it absolutely terrified me.

How could I leave the only career that I knew, the only way that I had developed to generate a significant revenue to support my family? I had not been fulfilling my true purpose, and life was letting me know that I could no longer put it off. This was my epiphany—my aha moment—and it was the beginning of living my life on purpose.

It took eighteen months from that point until I transitioned out of my job. On May 5th, 2013, I left my job and have never looked back.

NATALIE'S STORY

I have not had the same experience Reg described. I am still working in the occupation for which I went to school and received my education. But that does not mean that I have not had my own aha moments. In fact, Reg has been by my side through many of them, and continues to quietly smile when I experience small divine winks as I continue to stay on course, walking in my purpose. Sometimes she even blatantly points them out to me, almost as if she is hitting me over the head with a proverbial frying pan!

I continue to be a work in progress, but one of my most memorable moments occurred when I discovered how important connection is to me. I was preparing for a TEDx audition, and I had what I thought was a brilliant idea to combine my background in audiology and the concepts of "listening" versus "hearing"—how I can uniquely connect the concept from one's ear to his or her purpose. I was struggling to formulate my concept when one of my best friends, Dr. Tiffany Brown, a fellow audiologist as well as someone who happens to own her own speaking coach company, Level Up Consulting, posed one simple question and left me to focus and ponder.

She asked, "Why is this topic so important for you to share with others?" I proceeded to think through why I was so passionate about talking about the idea of connection, and while thoughts flooded my brain and tears began to pour down my face, I realized my why. I knew that people were important to me. I knew that I was kind to people. I knew that I didn't treat people terribly behind closed doors. I knew that I didn't use people. I knew that I didn't take on responsibilities just because they made me look good but instead because I believed in the cause. I knew that I didn't like to be compared to people who were superficial. I knew that I need to surround myself with people who are good, kind, supportive, and real. I knew that I wanted to stay real and be real, because real happens based on connection. I knew that what I knew about listening, along with my passion for connection, could build strong relationships.

Remembering these pivotal moments helps us become more of who we are. When we pause to take the time to recall our stories, those stories become the basis for how we truly connect with others.

UNDERSTANDING THE HERO'S JOURNEY

Movies and stories often follow a storytelling template called "The Hero's Journey." It involves a hero who goes on an adventure, and in a critical-decision moment, the hero overcomes a crisis and returns home transformed. During the journey, there is an epiphany or aha moment that leads the hero to victory and, ultimately, transformation.

If you've ever read a Marvel or DC comic book or watched one of the franchise's movies, you likely know the hero's journey very well. Look at the story of Batman: He was an orphaned boy whose parents were shot and killed when he was a child. He's wealthy, raised by the family butler. He struggles with the constant pull of both good and evil and the desire to seek revenge for his tragic loss by becoming a vigilante. He is tormented by his identity and the destruction of his family. Ultimately, he realizes that he can't go back and save his parents, but he can use his wealth to allow him to be Batman, protecting and saving Gotham and its residents from villains. This also affords him the opportunity to feel a morsel of revenge with each villain he takes down.

The epiphany is, he has a choice. He can be a hero who can make a difference in the lives of others and save them from the same fate as his parents, or he can wallow in his grief, seeking to find the people who murdered his parents and take revenge. Thereby, his epiphany leads to his transformation into Batman.

It's likely that we are hugely oversimplifying this particular hero's journey. In actuality, there are numerous journeys and epiphanies in each of the various story lines for the Batman character, but we're reaching for the highest journey for the character himself, not the various stories connected to his life. So, all you true comic buffs out there, you are welcome to pick apart our given example, but we think most readers will understand what we've tried to demonstrate through it. Epiphanies are a necessary part of our growth journey. Without them, we meander through places of uncertainty, never quite finding ourselves.

WHY ARE EPIPHANIES SO IMPORTANT TO GROWTH?

Our friend Holly Dowling asks a question during every interview on her podcast, "Celebration of You": "What was your defining moment? The moment that caused a major shift in your life and that possibly led you down the path that you're on." Holly asks this question because she knows that at the crux of every personal story, especially stories of personal success and overcoming, there is a moment where an individual wants something different in their lives. These defining moments are our growth moments in life. The hero is always looking for the opportunity to grow, to transform into the best version of himself or herself. The epiphany is critical to the hero's growth and ability to move forward into their grandest opportunity. Without the epiphany, the hero (you) can't move toward a plan to go beyond conflict and remains unresolved within self.

Epiphanies are usually clarifying moments wherein we experience a sudden realization of why we haven't been able to get unstuck from a certain place in life. This insight forces us to see something about ourselves that we couldn't see before. They allow us to have a breakthrough. However, the epiphany alone cannot cause the change that is needed to experience transformation. Once the hero experiences an epiphany, he or she must then take action to actually reach the breakthrough and experience a true transformation. It requires having the courage and resolve to push through the problem and implement changes that turn the epiphany into transformation.

THE PSYCHOLOGY OF AHA MOMENTS

According to a recent study conducted by Drexel University's Creative Research Lab, our aha moments can actually trigger a rush of pleasure in the brain. For some people, when they have an insightful moment it causes the brain to generate high-frequency gamma activity immediately after the aha that results in feelings similar to the neural reward signals triggered by sexual gratification, certain foods, a thirst-quenching drink, or other pleasure-centered experiences. Why is this important? Well, the research also suggests that, "The fact that some people find insight experiences to be highly pleasurable reinforces the notion that insight can be an intrinsic reward for problem solving and comprehension that makes use of the same reward circuitry in the brain that processes rewards from addictive drugs, sugary foods, or love."

What does this all mean? If we can learn to seek and harness the power of aha moments then we may be able to use them to motivate us to continue to take action, reaching our goals, and moving closer to the dreams that we have in our hearts. The power of an epiphany can help you to solve the problems that you encounter on the journey to reaching your dreams. This can be instrumental in keeping you on track, regardless of the challenges that you encounter. Why? Because if you know that taking moments of solitude and mindfulness to seek insight from within will ultimately lead you to a solution, then you will always know that your breakthrough will certainly be found.

Imagine how different things can be if you know with certainty that regardless of challenges or setbacks, you WILL eventually succeed. You wouldn't give up and you would continuously take action knowing that your own insight will lead you to reach your goals and dreams.

Are you reading this and wondering if you have experienced a moment like this? Trust us. If you start to be more open to trusted conversations with others and yourself, you will see them more often. Maybe you have experienced something, but you weren't aware of the lesson to be learned. Maybe you have to push yourself out of a comfortable environment in order propel into new experiences with opportunities to learn, grow, and transform. One of the best ways to encourage epiphany moments is to practice sitting quietly using meditation or journaling to focus your mind on a particular issue that you are trying to overcome. Become highly aware of yourself, your energy, your breathing, and the power of your existence. Seek the revelation that you need to solve your current issue, and know that, eventually, you will have insight that will lead you there.

What is currently holding you back from taking action on something that you know is important in order to live your life to the fullest? Until you have your own aha moment, you won't be able to move fully past the wall preventing you from moving forward. Once you experience the aha moment, the next step is committing to the changes necessary to turn the epiphany into the transformation.

Chapter Review

- Epiphanies, or aha moments, come suddenly. They allow you to have deeper insight into something that you already know. They are usually the catalyst for a breakthrough, and they are needed to make a change or improvement in your life.
- Almost every movie or fictional story has a built-in epiphany moment for the character in which he or she finally sees how to become the hero of the story.
- When you have an epiphany moment, you MUST take immediate action in order to leverage it for transformation.
- There is a psychological affect that epiphanies have on us, they actually trigger pleasure centers in the brain which can be effective in motivating us to continue taking action.

Time to ACT!

Today's Date:

Assess – Journal about what you wish to take action on related to this chapter's topic.

Commit – Write down the action you are willing to commit to in the next twelve months.

Transform – Identify an actionable goal that will transform the commitment into a measurable outcome.

CHAPTER FIVE

IT'S SO HARD TO SAY GOODBYE (CHANGE)

"The secret to change is to focus all of your energy, not on fighting the old, but on building the new."
—Socrates

NATALIE'S STORY

Sometimes, in order to move forward, you have to leave people behind. This is not a bad thing; it is honest. It is healthy. It can be good to break free from repetitive behaviors and work procedures, from toxic relationships, and especially from environments and obligations that do no align with your core values and beliefs. Change is inevitable at times. We have all experienced situations that led up to change, situations that possibly included leaving jobs, leaving people, and leaving environments. In my lifetime, I have also found that, in order to connect better to what I need to do, I have to learn to disconnect. As a person who enjoys and thrives through connection, disconnecting is difficult, but necessary, as it implies that you have to fully shut people out in order for you to focus or to move ahead on a clear path.

Change is not easy, but it can and has to be done. Everyone experiences change, but how do you react to it? Some people don't do well with change, but it will still happen. Some will not understand the reason why things have to change, but that unfortunately doesn't matter. Again, I don't say these things to be flippant but because change is hard, and it continues to happen, over and over. With every change, we need to learn and gauge the way we react.

REGEANIE'S STORY

Change is ALWAYS unsettling for me because it forces me to deal with unknowns and honestly, it forces me to confront fears. Like many, I like to know what is coming next. I like to know that when I go into my kitchen in the mornings, I will find my usual "go to" items in the places that I keep them. Sometimes I become a creature of habit because habit aligns with what I know and am comfortable with. However, I never allow myself to get stuck indefinitely because I am unwilling to change. I've learned over the years that each change, though uncomfortable, makes room for growth and improvement in my life. These changes also pave the way for greater opportunity to live in my truth and to create profound peace.

Probably the most challenging changes in my life were going through divorce. I have been divorced twice and each time it was so extremely difficult that I hesitated for long periods of time before making the decision and taking the necessary action. During my second divorce, I had very small children and had the extra burden of dealing with the guilt associated with dragging them through change as well. I had to learn that making these difficult decisions leading to unwanted change was in the long run the best decisions for all involved, but it didn't make the process of going through the changes any easier. Sometimes knowing the need for change isn't enough to make the change, but I found that believing in my ability to lead myself, one step at a time through the change, gave me the courage to do, even in the face of my fears.

Why is change so scary and hard to accept? Is it the way you frame your thinking? How do you feel about—and furthermore, react to—change?

CHANGE IS INEVITABLE

A good example is the aging process. We don't want our kids to grow up and not need us or move out. But those realities are inevitable. We don't want to grow older because doing so means we have is less and less time on this earth to do what we were placed here to do. But doing so is inevitable. Therefore, how do we deal with it?

As easy or hard as these words may be, we must "suck it up, buttercup" and make the most of it. We must be aware of what comes with each change and be proactive. We must instill in our children the importance of who they choose to hang out with, who will help mold our children so that if and when they don't turn to us, they turn to those individuals. We must be proactive with our health—getting older comes with a lesser functioning of just about everything—so how do we make ourselves stronger? Healthier?

CHANGE IS GOOD

We choose to change because we believe the new choice is and will be better for us and our families. Don't stop believing this to be true. We have been involved in many situations where we have had to make the difficult decision to leave. Sometimes, these aren't our favorite decisions, but they need to be made.

Natalie has moved five times in twenty-four years of marriage, and although some moves were harder than others, she can confidently say that each move happened at the perfect time for her family and didn't inhibit her professional growth. Rather, it allowed her to grow professionally.

Other times, the decision to leave was easier once she identified a toxic individual or environment that caused her health to decline and her stress levels to increase, made her bitter and angry, and tore down her self-confidence. Although these departures were emotional, in retrospect they were difficult because the people and environments hid their ugly sides well. In addition, she allowed her brain to think that if her choice to leave didn't make sense to observers, perhaps she was wrong or too sensitive. Over time, she's been glad to see that all the hurt and deflation she encountered from these difficult decisions led to faster discernment of red flags. She is now able to read between the lines more clearly and further develop her experiences into her core values, which, in turn, helps her much more carefully make decisions as to whether or not to get involved in something.

CHANGE IS SAYING GOODBYE

Sometimes in order to move forward, you have to leave people and things behind. It isn't easy, but disconnecting and growing into discernment is necessary, especially if you are so comfortable that you do not recognize that change needs to happen in order for there to be growth. It may be hard to sit where you are and enjoy the moment before the change, but we encourage you not to look back and be sad that a moment or event is over. Instead, be glad and feel blessed that it happened.

Other times, you knew deep down that change was the right decision, but the backlash from people who didn't understand your decision may have been difficult. In either situation, you choose the change, and you can also choose to be intentional about keeping in touch with those who are left behind. Worst-case scenario? Maybe you recognize after the fact that a particular change wasn't the right one to make. So, you learn, pivot, and build character. Even if this happens, sometimes the only way you would have come to know what was right and what wasn't was to go through it. You must learn from everything, and sometimes those lessons are not just thought about or read, they're personally experienced.

CHANGE IS WALKING INTO THE UNKNOWN

Sometimes we don't fully see the results of change when we are going through the process. You may anticipate change because you have an idea to create something new and grow, but feel fearful about stepping into that idea. Question: Do you truly believe that if you were to create the idea, at least ONE person would benefit? Is that alone worth it to you? If so, build your confidence and strength by taking action toward the next logical steps.

Some of the hardest parts of change that we have encountered are the fear of the unknown, the judgement of others, and the building up of a new support system. We have learned to be both mentally and emotionally strong while quickly building and leaning on our inner circles for strength and constant encouragement. We used to think that we had many close friends, but an inner circle of people we could count on one hand, and who we can trust completely has allowed us to accept change and embrace it each time it happens.

Have you ever wondered why so many people desire to change in some area of their lives, but for some reason, simply can't seem to make those changes no matter how hard they try?

If you are on the road to growth, understand that the process involves change. You have to sacrifice. You have to let go of certain parts of your personality, which can be difficult. We are so used to doing things or thinking about things a certain way. It's scary to let go of the things we are familiar with, and the thought of doing so can lead to worries about what we stand to lose.

Attachment to the harmful mindset that you can "coast through life" only by relying on your past successes is an illusion. Your skill sets erode over time. Eventually, you reach a point where you don't even know what to do to produce any kind of result. The way to exit this dilemma is to understand that the world rewards action right here, right now. Not tomorrow, the day after, or next week. Right here, right now.

Let's start working with what you already have and examining what is already within you. This is the first step. Ask yourself this question: What is really important? It should be clear to you which of the things you do on a day-to-day basis are important. If you need more clarity, start by asking yourself, "Does this move my career forward? Does this help my business in a profound way? Does this push me closer to my life goals?"

You may be thinking to yourself that as long as you can tie any of your routine to your life goals, you should continue doing them. Not so fast. You also need to test your life goals. Are you assuming that certain goals are your life goals? Change includes re-examining goals and asking yourself whether or not the objectives are really all that important to you. Is this what you really want out of life? A lot of people actually haven't bothered to ask themselves these questions. They tend to go on autopilot, and if they do manage to achieve those grand objectives, they end up not being what they're looking for after all. Re-examine your life goals, and don't be afraid to ask yourself if you truly still want them. Maybe you need to refocus and redefine.

We love Mel Robbins! If you don't know who she is, Google "5-Second Rule" and you will find her. Regeanie first read her book in 2017, thinking the concept seemed way too simple. How could one transform his or her life with a 5-second countdown?

She honestly didn't believe it but decided to give it a try, and guess what? It truly changed her life. Things on which she had procrastinated on those with which she had stood in a place of fear started to fall away with the implementation of the 5-Second Rule. Apparently, there is science behind the principle of triggering the brain to do something different with a countdown.

Chapter one of Mel's book, *The 5 Second Rule: Transform Your Life, Work and Confidence with Everyday Courage*, is titled, "Five Seconds to Change Your Life" and it bears a quote that reads: "If you're searching for that one person who will change your life, look in the mirror." Ouch! You mean we can't continue to blame everyone and everything else for what isn't working in our lives and for the things that we are not accomplishing? That's right, even though we are known to frequently say, "It's not about you," in this case, *it is all about you!* You have to own your mess and commit to the changes needed to clean up that mess.

As part of the ACT Now movement, we encourage you to consider using the 5-Second Rule to transform your life. As an added twist to supplement the method, we want you to end your countdown with the trigger phrase "ACT Now!" That's right, every time you think about procrastinating, stalling, or giving in to fear and self-doubt, we want you to "5-4-3-2-1-ACT Now" your way to action. Why? Because the fastest way to command change is to put yourself into motion and take action. We are both truly thankful for Mel Robbins' honesty, transparency, relevance, and willingness to share with the world her mess as well as her solution to cleaning up that mess. Thanks, Mel!

UNDERSTANDING THE CHANGE CYCLE

Does the thought of creating change sound good logically but in practice make you want to run in the opposite direction? Have you ever wondered why accepting change isn't an easier process? Well, it can be if you choose to condition your mind to view change as a positive necessity to growth in life. It's also important to be realistic with yourself and accept that change does require significant effort and commitment, but when the outcome outweighs the pain of changing (or not changing), you can begin to more easily implement the desired change.

Most people want to make positive changes in their lives. The desire exists, but somewhere between identifying the desire and engaging in actual execution, breakdown occurs, and they abandon any goal attached to change. The reasons why so many of us don't follow through on the changes necessary to achieve our goals is that we are often afraid, either consciously or subconsciously, of the changes that must occur in order to achieve a given goal.

We all experience this change cycle; it is very predictable. If you examine your past experiences with goal setting, looking specifically at those areas where you abandoned a goal, it is highly likely that you can insert your scenario into this cycle. When we first heard about this concept, we could see the pattern repeatedly in areas where we had struggled with goal attainment.

Let's first discuss what the cycle looks like. There are six (6) phases to the change cycle:

The first is DISCONTENTMENT. This is where you identify something in your life that needs to change. You want a better result or outcome, and the only way that you will get it is to make a change. You realize you're discontent, however you tolerate things the way that they are because it has become your normal. So, even though you would like to make a change, there isn't enough motivation yet to cause you to execute a change.

Then there comes a time where you can no longer accept whatever it is that is making you discontent. You've had enough and decide that it's time to take action. It is time to make a change and work towards the outcome you desire. This is phase two, the BREAKING POINT. Sometimes the breaking point is self-initiated, but other times it is forced upon us by external circumstances. Something happens, possibly something life-altering, unexpected, or out of our control. Whatever the case may be, it causes us to decide that it is time for a change.

As soon as you make the DECISION to change, which is phase three, you immediately trigger your reptilian brain, the "lizard" brain, which is responsible for primitive brain functions, namely basic needs like procreation, food, and fear. It also controls instinct and self-preservation.

Because your subconscious brain generally evaluates change as a threat, it immediately senses FEAR (which is phase 4 of the cycle) and goes into self-preservation mode. Its job is to quickly convince you that whatever you're contemplating is a really bad idea, and you shouldn't do it. Period. You start to assess all that is connected to the change—physical, mental, and emotional—and almost inevitably, more pain is perceived to be associated with the change than pleasure. Meaning, you are more fearful of what the change will bring than you are committed to the outcome that the change will bring. If this fear overrules and the lizard brain has its way, you will move into the next phase, which is AMNESIA. As a coping mechanism, the brain allows itself to forget the pain that led to the breaking point. It doesn't want to confront the pain or discomfort of change, and it blocks out what you wanted to change in the first place, or at least it blocks out the strong desire for change. This protection mechanism becomes a form of self-sabotage.

This leads to the final phase of the cycle, phase 6, which is BACKTRACKING. You go back to whatever action, behavior, or pattern you wanted to change. Maybe it's old habits, or addictions, or even relationships.

It is also in this stage that you may introduce competing commitments. These are commitments that are counter-productive to your goals and prevent you from staying committed to them. For example, you shop when you know that you really don't need to and shouldn't because it goes against your budgeting goals. You know deep inside that you often go shopping as a way to escape how you are feeling. After all, it helps you feel better in the moment. You manage to do well for a couple of months. You don't spend money on wants, only on needs, and you are improving your overall spending habits. Then it happens. You have a bad day, and the first thing you think about is how much better you feel when you go shopping for something that you really want. You find yourself at the local mall or store purchasing the item that you really would like to have. The rush feels good, so you make the purchase.

A couple of days later, you realize that you feel worse than you did before making your purchase. But now, all of your savings are depleted. You've been here before; it always ends the same way. You tell yourself that you aren't going to allow it to happen again. Yet, a couple of months later, you are right back in the same scenario. This is a change cycle that will keep occurring until you truly commit to the changes needed to completely break free.

Your lizard brain tells you that the changes needed are going to impact you negatively, and fear sets in. You forget about the remorse you felt the last time you blew through all of your money trying to make yourself feel better. And, you start to identify rationalizations as to why you need to have the ability to spend as you please. These rationalizations become competing commitments that fight against your true goal of reducing spending on wants and improving your overall financial health. This time, however, it's worse because you have a financial obligation you can't meet because you overspent. You then begin the cycle all over again.

The thing is this: If you don't follow through on the change and break the cycle, the cycle will only continue to repeat itself. Except, each time you cycle through, the breaking point is going to get worse, because you are going to feel worse each time. At some point, you will have to face extreme discomfort from the cycle. This is usually the time that you'd break the cycle, but because breaking the cycle is typically more painful than following through with the old pattern, you don't. Half the battle is understanding the cycle so that you can take steps necessary to break it.

The other important step is becoming honest with yourself—extremely honest. In a journal or on a piece of paper, identify where you have been stuck in the change cycle and what sacrifice(s) you have made as a result of not breaking the cycle. What haven't you accomplished because of the cycle? What are the things that you've wanted to change for a long time? What things have you tried to change but gave up on before you actually made the change? How has this impacted your life? What things have you been settling for because you've been unable to break the cycle?

It really comes down to you deciding that your desire for a different outcome outweighs your fear of change. This will help you to stop the cycle once and for all. It's really up to you to make the choice. Are you going to do things differently? Or continue experiencing the cycle, with each time being worse than the last? Just remember, you always have a choice, and until you commit to doing things differently, you will experience the same outcome. Albert Einstein once said, "The definition of insanity is doing the same thing over and over again and expecting different results." Are you stuck in a cycle, repeating the same patterns over again and expecting a different result? If so, now is the time to take action toward change.

We did not develop the foundational information for the "Change Cycle," and we want to give credit to Natalie and Joel Rivera of the Transformation Academy for their work in this area as part of their life coaching programs.

Chapter Review

- Change is not easy, but it can and has to be done.
- Sometimes in order to move forward, you have to leave people and things behind.
- Accepting change can be easier if you condition your mind to view change as a positive necessity to help you grow in life.
- You need to follow through in order to change and break the cycle or it will repeat itself, and each time you will feel worse.
- Change comes down to being honest with yourself, along with the decision that your desire for the outcome outweighs your fear of the change.

Time to ACT!

Today's Date:

Assess – Journal about what you wish to take action on related to this chapter's topic.

Commit – Write down the action you are willing to commit to in the next twelve months.

Transform – Identify an actionable goal that will transform the commitment into a measurable outcome.

CHAPTER SIX

DOING WHAT IT TAKES (COMMITMENT)

"There are only two options regarding commitment; you're either in or you're out. There's no such thing as life in between."
—Pat Riley

NATALIE'S STORY

I was once told that someone asked about me, "When will Natalie ever stop fishing?"

I happened to be in a short-lived environment with only somewhat supportive colleagues. I say that because they seemed supportive at first, but they also wanted to keep me in a place in which I was useful for them. I was in an unusual space. On one hand, my audiology career had taken off, and I was hired to be a director due to my experience and expertise. I was hired to help with the communication and branding of hearing healthcare with a mission of educating consumers to increase the percentage of people actually seeking help for their hearing needs.

I ended up trying to educate businesses and salespeople on how to communicate effectively with audiologists. I soon discovered that many in that audience were not as interested in connecting and understanding audiologists and their business needs as they were about the sales numbers.

On the other hand, I started to discover that, in addition to my knowledge and expertise in audiology outside of my "day job," I was beginning to learn how to use digital communication to truly connect to people, and I enjoyed watching their businesses grow. At the time, others were seeing it as well, and I was even offered a position as a Director of Communication in a global women's entrepreneurial organization. I didn't know what it all meant, but I knew that I was enjoying this other avenue of connecting to people.

Although it made me angry and upset that people did not understand my journey, and I believed that if I branched out into something that I did not go to school for I would look and seem "scatterbrained" because I kept "fishing" for other things to do, I also tried to step back to see what my reaction was truly all about. Over time, I allowed myself to be okay with stepping into something that I was good at doing. Reg was a big guiding factor for me. She saw and believed in me more deeply than the words and thoughts I kept speaking to myself and helped me look at it from a more strategic standpoint of why this form of connection came so easily for me. She helped me see that being good at something new and unexpected could also mean I needed to expand what I was doing as an audiologist. My experience and expertise connecting people using hearing and communication might also allow me to use my way of connecting and my experience of connecting to others through a digital world to introduce people and businesses to each other and to their consumers.

Clarity helped drive me stronger and deeper into commitment. I had to commit and create goals to continue to build and grow. I had to commit to not pay attention to the noise around me and to show up for what I knew I could deliver. This started in the way I shaped my year and what Reg and I committed to do to start off our year.

Like any other year, we started off this year by choosing a "Word of the Year" with a goal of living out the word. I started this process in 2016, based on the Inc.com article "One Word Can Change Your Life in 2016. Here's How" by Minda Zetlin, co-author of *The Geek Gap*. For the next four years, I encouraged others to do the same and then tried to hold them accountable by reaching out and checking in on their chosen "word of the year." This year was extra special. This year, I was challenged not only to choose a word but also to take it a step further and create an acronym using my word. Also, this was the year when Regeanie and I chose the same word and only discovered that when we shared it with each other. The word was ACTION.

ACTION leads to RESULTS. Another way to say that is, results are only possible when you decide to take action. Results are what make you feel accomplished and help take you to the next step on the road to success. Success is defined by what you do, not what you may dream about, your potential, your hopes, or your wishes. Everybody's got those, and anybody can daydream. But to actually achieve your dreams and live a life of purpose, you have to take action. You can't live a life of purpose by doing nothing. You have to believe that in order to achieve happiness and joy, you have to TAKE ACTION.

REGEANIE'S STORY

When I think of commitment, besides my husband and Natalie, I am reminded of my friendship with actress, singer, entrepreneur, and philanthropist, Dawnn Lewis. We met in 2017 through a mutual acquaintance, and I had the opportunity to work with her on establishing her 501(c)3 nonprofit, A New Day Foundation (https://anewdayfoundation.net). Dawnn is an amazing person, and her level of commitment to everything that she does is extraordinary. During our first conversation, we hit it off immediately. One thing was very clear in that initial meeting was that her level of commitment to her work and her desire to give back to young people were unlike that of many people with whom I'd worked up until that point.

A funny side note: When she first set up her initial consultation call with me, I didn't connect the dots in terms of who she was. I kept thinking to myself that her name was familiar, but honestly, it just didn't click. Once we were on the call and I heard her voice, it clicked because I was a huge fan of "A Different World" in the late '80s and early '90s, in which she played the character Jaleesa Vinson. I tried really hard not to focus on who she was but on getting her the results that she needed. This level of commitment to the process actually helped me to better understand her commitment and discipline in both life and business. In turn, it has made me extremely committed to helping people who don't have a lot of time to waste and need to get the quick results they are looking for.

Dawnn has done some wonderful things through her nonprofit to help better the lives of underserved youth and improve their opportunities to go to college and experience opportunities in the entertainment and media fields. I am grateful for my friendship with her, and she is a constant role model for me when it comes to the importance of staying committed to your goals and dreams as well as being committed to your own success and the success of others. She is a perfect example of someone who has taken action regardless of fears or challenges, and she continues to embody the persona of someone who is always willing to ACT Now!

ACTION begins with a COMMITMENT and a DECISION. A lot of people downplay the importance of making decisions. Many of us think that decisions are automatic, that we only need to see the benefits for ourselves and the decision will naturally flow. Benefits to change don't happen overnight, but they only happen by making a decision. For example, a diet. Or a new job or promotion. If you are focusing on making a change, it will likely come as no surprise that you may fail if you do not work on the decisions you have to make every day to lead to the change. One of the most powerful steps to personal success is a conscious decision.

We couldn't just choose it and not hold each other accountable. We started meeting by phone at least once a month to share our goals, our fears, our wins, and our struggles. We also created and facilitated a mastermind group of our own friends and savvy business entrepreneurs where we could leverage each other's strengths and ideas to propel us forward even more. (We will talk more about masterminds in chapter ten).

The power of choice is one of the single most important personal powers that you have. Do not assume that it is always in play or that you have exercised it. When you are conscious about your choice to get things done now, it leads you to commitment. Two things are happening: You are CHOOSING to do things and you're choosing to do them now. These must flow together.

COMMIT TO GET THINGS DONE

First, decide that you will step up the quantity of your output. Whether you a salesperson, a lawyer, a doctor, a medical professional, a janitor, a business owner, or anything else, you have to do more. You have to commit to producing more output. You have to also commit to following through until the task is completed. It is easy to get distracted, but it is important to get things done so you can focus your time and energy on the next thing that needs to get done. Granted, there are some things that you may be able to multi-task, but on the big actions, you sometimes have to focus completely on them to make sure they get done. Being able to check off something on your to-do list can provide you with the confidence and sense of accomplishment necessary to take on the next big task.

COMMIT TO PRODUCE MEASURABLE RESULTS

You have to be able to measure your efforts by quantifying outcomes. Focus on your consumers in terms of number of sales or look at website views, visitors, and engagement. Whatever you are delivering, you have to produce results that are quantifiable. If you don't know where to start, try starting by setting SMART goals (we discuss SMART goals and the goal setting process in chapter eight). Once you are more familiar with the practice of tracking and measuring goals, you will want to create consistent results that you can measure!

COMMIT TO BOOST QUALITY

Many people are under the impression that just because they are able to produce daily, they are doing well. We wish it were that simple. If you produce substandard work, it doesn't really matter whether you replicate it a million times, as it will still be substandard work. Personal effectiveness involves improving the quality of your output. For example, if you are in sales, each contract you close must be worth more than the previous contract or sale. If you are a store owner, the quality of the brands and clientele that you are attracting must be elevated. That's how you know you're challenging yourself and improving. Many people are too eager to skate through without focusing on quality. They may believe that as long as they can rack up high numbers, that is good enough. This is not true. It takes commitment to rise and challenge yourself to increase the quality of your output.

COMMIT TO FOCUS ON THE BIG GOALS

Becoming a more effective person leads to being a more purposeful person. You're not just hitting numbers because you have a quota to fill. You're not just seeing as many patients as you can as fast as you can because you can't wait until you are able to hit the golf links. Going through the motions does not allow you to become the most effective and caring person you could be, because there is no underlying reason for you to fulfill that goal. You have to COMMIT. What's the point of cranking out sales when it doesn't lead to anything meaningful in your life? What's the point in studying when it doesn't help you accomplish a big goal in your life? Figuring out what to do and how to do it is not as important as understanding why you're doing it. You have to be motivated by the "why" because the sense of urgency, focus, and purpose will give you the power and the immediacy you need not only to increase the quantity and quality of your work but also help you withstand negativity, discouragement, and setbacks.

Big goals in your life are personal. This makes it tricky, because while they may be very deep and meaningful to you, they might not mean much to the next person. It is your job to zero in on these big goals because not only are they are part of your personal truths, you should be able to benefit from the sense of emotional urgency that they produce.

REGEANIE'S STORY

This year, I realized that I needed to implement some additional business models into the nonprofit that I founded. It is a training and development nonprofit whose mission is to develop strong leaders for business and community engagement. We provide training and coaching services to underserved individuals, and in our first few years, we have relied primarily on grants, sponsorships, and donations to fund the organization. While we enjoyed a small amount of earned income, I realized we were really missing an opportunity to generate more income to sustain the mission as well as have greater impact in the world.

This change in our business model required that I seek a business coach to carry out the technical side of the business model changes. I was introduced to Chad Fullerton of Fullerton Media, Inc. in the earlier part of the year, and I started working with him to map out a plan. He is an amazing entrepreneur and marketing expert who has helped me stay committed to the process of delivering great digital products to multiply my impact and the impact of others in the world. He has been committed to our organization's results, ensuring that we can measure the value of our work together. I am grateful that he has remained committed to the success of my vision, even when I've had doubts.

It is absolutely impossible to reach goals and dreams without commitment! There is your own commitment, and additionally, there is the commitment of those who believe in you and want to see you succeed. However, if you are unable to commit, you can't expect others to show up to support the vision. Commitment MUST start with you!

COMMIT TO SET A TIMELINE OF INTENTION

At this point, you should understand why you need to decide and COMMIT to being more effective. However, the challenge is that the decision to be effective and an understanding of the reasons why you should be effective do not help you all that much. Until you feel a sense of urgency, all of this will be 'in theory" to you. All these insights alone will not push your life forward. It is kind of like going to a seminar where you are supplied with very interesting information, but at the end of the day, the information in a vacuum does not move your life forward. You are not able to use the information itself to change the way you look at yourself or at your place in life. If we don't allow the things that we learn with our minds to sync with the level of our hearts and our passions, nothing is going to lead us to commit to change.

This is why timelines help. Timelines take the theory or the possibility of change and convert it into cold, hard reality. You are no longer playing around, and start acting more intentional. You do not allow your feelings to dictate when you should get your act together. You no longer play games where you say that you will only take action "when the timing is right." Most importantly, when you set timelines to boost your personal effectiveness, you are no longer waiting for other people. The more you wait, the more ineffective you are. Commit to setting a timeline to start acting more intentionally right here, right now.

COMMIT TO SET THE RIGHT TIME TO START

Be careful not to make the common mistake of giving yourself too much time. Especially when you are excited about setting a time right now, be aware of whether or not the deadline you have selected may be too far in the future. If you set a deadline that is too far in the future, chances are, you may forget about the goal, become busy with other tasks, or have a change in priorities. Your calendar may fill up so much in the meantime that by the time the deadline arrives, you will find yourself completely unprepared.

Don't give yourself too much advanced notice. The deadline has to be close enough to the present that you can remain focused on the start date along with the why. On the other hand, a problem with setting the start date so close to the present date is that you end up intimidating yourself. Try not to set your start date so close to the present day that you end up with anxiety, guilt, or disappointment. You may be setting yourself up to fail and find yourself intimidated by what you need to do and the changes that you need to go through. This can lead to being afraid of the work that's involved, at which point you'll get thrown off track. Instead, try to shoot for a reasonable time period. Too long of a deadline may lead to a lost sense of emotional urgency, and too imminent of a deadline may cause to you to essentially freeze because you're intimidated.

- Without commitment we would not have our relationship and friendship.
- Without commitment we would not have experienced opportunities.
- Without commitment, we would not have been able to live out our word: ACTION.

CHALLENGE: Which of the six areas of commitment do you need to work on? Can you choose at least three to take on?

Chapter Review

- Success is defined by what you do, not what you dream about, your potential, your hopes or your wishes.
- ACTION BEGINS with COMMITMENT and a DECISION.

- COMMITMENT means you are choosing to do things AND you're choosing to do them now. These must flow together.
- Becoming a more effective person means becoming a more purposeful person.

Time to ACT!

Today's Date:

Assess – Journal about what you wish to take action on related to this chapter's topic.

Commit – Write down the action you are willing to commit to in the next twelve months.

Transform – Identify an actionable goal that will transform the commitment into a measurable outcome.

CHAPTER SEVEN

JUST DO IT...NOW! (DISCIPLINE)

"Discipline is the bridge between goals and accomplishment."
—Jim Rohn

NATALIE'S STORY

I have no problem with discipline. In fact, I sometimes use the tagline "tiger mom" when I am pushing discipline with my kids. Of course, it is easy when you can take away a phone for a messy room or not allow a friend to stay over or bench a kid from sports for poor grades or a poor attitude. But when it comes to discipline in taking action in my own life…well…that is another story.

I am one of those people who keeps busy. So busy, sometimes, that I am not disciplined enough to spend time on my own things—so much so that it can occasionally make me exhausted and overwhelmed. So much so that I use the excuse of being so busy in order not to spend time with people or tasks or goals that need to be tended to.

On the other hand, I have found that at certain times I can sit down and be very disciplined. Most of the time, it is when I am in the beginning of a project. I have the spark, the fire, the drive, and I am motivated to reach the outcome. Slowly, over time, this can fade for me. I have found that as time continues to roll on, my discipline gets weaker. I let things sit for longer. I believe that it is important for me to be aware of what can get me hyped up again in order to be productive.

This might not work for everyone, as there are different ways people can turn on and off that switch, but for me, taking action and being disciplined is quickly sparked if I make a promise to someone or have a deadline in sight. If I say I am going to get something done, my integrity is hugely important to me. I have found that keeping promises and overdelivering on a deadline early ignites my desire and action to return to being disciplined.

REGEANIE'S STORY

Unlike Natalie, implementing discipline into my life didn't come easily. Maybe it has a little bit to do with not having sports in my life, whereas she did. I've always looked at sports as a great way to develop relentless discipline. I've always admired those who are so dedicated and disciplined that they will claw their way through the deepest, darkest, hardest challenges to accomplish their goals.

While discipline is no longer something that completely evades me, I do from time to time have to be reminded of its importance when it comes to living to my highest potential. Over the years, I've had to hire coaches and mentors to bring accountability and discipline into my life in order to ensure that I would become the person that my success was waiting for. Danelle Delgado is one such person who forced me to double-down on the discipline needed to become the person that I desired to be.

Danelle is an amazing business mentor and coach who works with business owners and entrepreneurs around the world who wish to elevate to their highest potential. The author of *I Choose Joy*, she is known by those she works with as the Velvet Hammer (because her "soft" and nurturing personality hits hard in those areas where her clients need to improve) and the Millionaire Maker (because of the number of people she has worked with whose results include seven figures in business revenue growth).

I will never forget the impact that Danelle's famous tagline had on my life: "You have to be the one that your results require." These words resonated with me so deeply because they forced me to recognize that I can't rely on anyone else to drive my results; only I can do that. This, my friends, requires me to implement disciplines in my life like never before. It's no longer a discussion of what I "feel" like doing but rather a discussion of what I "must" do to achieve the results that I want to achieve.

Discipline needs both action and consistency. Discipline requires you to improve performance and time management and put a plan in place. One of the biggest reasons that we are unable to take action is procrastination driven by fear, overwhelm, and/or lack of discipline. We've discussed how fear plays a key role in preventing us from taking action as well as the overwhelm that comes from not setting clear goals that allow you to stay focused. Now let's discuss the role that discipline plays in taking action and accomplishing your goals.

Discipline and willpower are actually two sides of the same coin. Being honest with yourself about this simple area of your life can help drive you to become a more powerful, impressive, and successful version of yourself. Discipline comes down to the ability to control your own emotions and actions. As a child, this is a hard thing to do. However, over time, maturity takes over and it gets easier. But, even as adults, many things play into whether or not we are able to stay in control. Frustration, fatigue, failure, and even laziness come into play on occasion. We don't want to work late at night or through the night because it doesn't feel good, while closing our eyes and relaxing does. Even if we try to fight those desires on occasion, our minds fight us every step of the way. But, if we can learn better discipline, we will be able to curb the feeling of being a slave to the feelings that make us quit.

The disciplined individual has learned to simply tell themselves that it doesn't matter whether they like it or not; it has to be done, and that is the end of the conversation. They are able to focus on one goal or objective and shut out all other distracting thoughts and impulses that surface.

Developing laser focus on what you are doing is powerful because it allows you to complete your tasks. It also creates an agreeable congruence in everything you say and do, which people notice. They see that you are not easily upset by things that pop up or that people say, you are not desperate to please, and you do not have difficulty making decisions. In contrast, you are decisive and able to be immune to life's concerns when you need to be focused.

Although you may not think they are connected, being a people pleaser can get in the way of being focused on the tasks at hand. Why do we often try to please as many people as we can? Because we want to be liked. This can lead us to make weak decisions that do not align with others and end up upsetting them. If emotions are what lead our conversations and disputes, it can get us in trouble, as it causes us to react badly in a conversation. These kinds of decisions and actions can escalate over time and further affect us, causing us to disconnect and not get done the things we need to get done, making our lives even more difficult.

How do we become a disciplined person who is able to rise above and be in control of our actions and reactions? The same way we approach and want to be better in anything else: through practice and training. Think of the discipline of a professional and high-performance athlete dedicated to be the best...in order to be the best, it takes a lot of practice and training.

Kobe Bryant, also known as the Black Mamba, was an extremely disciplined basketball player. He was known to be relentless while on the court during games, but this phenomenal discipline went far beyond the times when he was playing. When he made game mistakes or wanted to improve on an area of his game, he was relentless in practicing and re-watching game videos. He was up before anyone else in the morning and was often the last one on the court practicing. This commitment to discipline was fueled by his desire to be his best at the game. When he retired, he applied this same commitment and discipline to his love for storytelling.

Discipline is the "X-Factor" that will allow you to go after your dreams and the goals that support them in a way that will keep you on track and focused, even when you don't feel like doing the work that needs to be done. Discipline will help you to persevere and push through any real or perceived obstacle, and it will keep you in the "game" when you might otherwise feel like giving up or settling for less.

HOW TO GAIN UNSTOPPABLE DISCIPLINE

First, we have to recognize that lessons in discipline can exist in every moment. Don't believe us? Think about your decisions throughout the day, maybe even over the length of an hour, or even just ten minutes. Discipline lies in the choices we make every day. It is the conscious ability to focus on one thing and, consequently, shut out all other distractions.

Distraction is in fact procrastination, and procrastination is indeed distraction. For example, when someone is speaking to you, it is your job to concentrate and focus acutely and intently on what they are saying. In an office situation, when you should be working but are interested in what is happening or in conversations on the other side of the room, it is your job to ignore the urge to look up.

Exercise is a big area ripe for distraction. We all know we should exercise, but we get tired and start to think that we can just wait until the next day. It is our job to ignore those feelings and power through anyway. Discipline starts with attacking these distractions and the emotions they can cause to rise up in you.

Sometimes it is as easy as recognizing and accepting that, in some situations, your feelings really don't matter. In other words, as long as you're not hurting yourself, it really does not matter if you are just a little hungry, a little cold, a little bored, or a little tired. It doesn't matter if you believe you deserve a treat. Being disciplined—or, as people sometimes joke, "adulting"—is all about learning how to resist that urge and instead focus on those actions that help you accomplish your goals.

This kind of incidental training can make you more aware and turn your interactions and experiences into chances to develop and hone your focus and discipline. In addition, you can also set yourself up for further training opportunities if you keep this awareness throughout your routine.

Many people who have the ability to push themselves through strict discipline swear by this one: taking a cold shower. The ability to stand in a cold shower is a great example of pushing yourself, as it takes a huge amount of willpower and discipline. As you'd expect, your body and mind will fight you every step of the way. But you will be training and harnessing your willpower if you can force yourself into that cold water anyway. Another benefit of cold showers is that they help produce more testosterone, which in turn increases blood circulation and trains our immune systems.

Yet another example that we can all easily commit

to is making our bed every morning. This seems simple, but many don't do it! As Admiral William H. McRaven of the United States Navy stated in his 2014 graduation speech he delivered to the University of Texas as well as his #1 New York Times Bestseller book: Make Your Bed: Little Things That Can Change Your Life…and Maybe the World, "If you want to change the world, start off by making your bed. If you make your bed every morning, you will have accomplished the first task of the day. It will give you a small sense of pride, and it will encourage you to do another task, and another, and another. By the end of the day, that one task completed will have turned into many tasks completed. Making your bed will also reinforce the fact that little things in life matter. If you can't do the little things right, you'll never be able to do the big things right. If, by chance, you have a miserable day, you will come home to a bed that's made. That you made. And a made bed gives you encouragement that tomorrow will be better." As you can see, making your bed is a great habit, as it successfully motivates you, even when you are stressed and in a hurry, to get a sense of accomplishment before leaving the house. In turn, and possibly unbeknownst to you, this is great training to get yourself to do other things that you need to do.

THE IMPORTANCE OF REWARD

Let's look at the other side. Although it is important to be disciplined and fight procrastination, it is also important to step back and enjoy life as well. No one is 100 percent disciplined 100 percent of the time. They may strive to be and want to be, but it's not realistic. If you are too repressed and too strict, it can lead to more serious control and self-worth issues down the line.

In other words, don't forget to give yourself a reward from time to time, especially at set times and when you have worked towards and accomplished a goal.

Want to reward yourself with a treat while cutting back on unhealthy foods? Be okay with the reward, but maybe consider it only once you have been able to go a whole day while keeping your calorie total to or even under a certain amount. Want to take a break and kick back and enjoy a good book? Give yourself a goal to hit first, such as completing a certain amount of work.

Trust us. Giving yourself a reward for hitting a goal or for good behavior is a great way to continue to motivate yourself and to allow you to add a some fun and excitement into your life without completely giving up on being disciplined and strict.

One simple example of this might be with your daily work. If you normally start your day's work by getting a cup of tea and then having a chat, it's time to turn that on its head. From now on, you get the cup of tea and the chat as a reward for doing other good work. You're only allowed those rewards after you have completed X amount of work. This motivates you and allows you to work with fewer interruptions. The same goes for checking your phone. Put it on silent and allow yourself to check it once an hour for only five minutes. Doing this helps to prevent procrastination because your will power doesn't have to be strong enough to completely avoid ever doing whatever that "thing" is. Instead, it only has to be strong enough to hold off for a while.

One additional tool to assist in training yourself to stop procrastinating: meditate.

Meditation is essentially an exercise in discipline. It's the practice of trying to remove all distracting thoughts for a short period of time. By utilizing this skill, you can start to become far less easily controlled by stress, by tiredness, by hunger, or by other impulses. Meditation makes us far more disciplined as well as much less stressed and better able to concentrate and focus for long periods of time. Of course, that requires discipline in itself. Start with small five-minute sessions a few times a week, and build up from there!

Chapter Review

- Discipline is the control you have over your own emotions and actions.
- Discipline comes through practice and training.

- Sometimes discipline is recognizing that your feelings don't matter, and you have to resist the urge of distractions in order to finish a task or accomplish a goal.
- No one is going to be 100 percent disciplined for 100 percent of the time—give yourself a reward from time to time.

Time to ACT!

Today's Date:

Assess – Journal about what you wish to take action on related to this chapter's topic.

Commit – Write down the action you are willing to commit to in the next twelve months.

Transform – Identify an actionable goal that will transform the commitment into a measurable outcome.

CHAPTER EIGHT

I AIN'T TRYIN' TO BE A GOAL DIGGER (GOAL SETTING)

"Our goals can only be reached through a vehicle of a plan, in which we must fervently believe, and upon which we must vigorously act. There is no other route to success."
—Pablo Picasso

REGEANIE'S STORY

Goal setting has never come easy for me. I always looked up to those who seemed to be able to define goals easily and master the skill of checking goals regularly, celebrating their completion. However, in spite of my challenges with goal setting, I've never discounted its importance or given up on the process.

Admittedly, I have gone through times when I was inconsistent in the process, but as practice and time revealed, most of my challenges and frustrations came because I was not setting effective goals. Most times, they were too vague and didn't have a clear indicator of progress or completion.

I am much better at the goal setting process now, but there is always room for growth. What I have learned is that it helps to have people in your inner circle whom you can trust with your goals so they can cheer you on and keep you accountable. Natalie has been part of that inner-circle accountability in my life. She has helped me to focus on the importance of consistency in relationships and staying connected to my goals. We need people in our lives who can help provide strength where we are weak. It is because of our friendship and accountability pact that I have become a stronger goal setter.

Goal setting doesn't always come easily. Actually, many people struggle with consistently staying in the goal setting process. Consider how many individuals set New Year's resolutions (can anyone say goal?) and don't keep them. They get sixty to ninety percent in, and their momentum wanes, frustration sets in, and before they know it, they're giving up.

We all want success, but many of us lack the strength of discipline to stay in the process. We talked about discipline in the last chapter, now let's examine the goal setting process. First of all, success leaves clues, which means that we should look at what other successful individuals have consistently done to get the results attached to their success. One of the common activities that successful individuals participate in is habitual goal setting. This includes establishing clear and measurable goals, and identifying actionable activities that support one's dreams. It also includes reviewing your goals on a regular basis and having them so ingrained in your being that working towards the goals becomes second nature. It is also important to remember that there are many different ways to approach the act of goal setting. Which process you use isn't as important as having a process that you enjoy and can consistently follow.

We look at setting goals in many different ways. For short-term activities, or milestone attached to larger goals, Natalie focuses on a short "things to do TODAY" list. She adds these reminders into her calendar on her phone so that she will see them in the present. Even if it is a task that she can get done in just a few minutes, such as making a phone call or appointment, she still lists them. Why? Because she likes to be able to delete them once they are completed. The feeling of crossing something off of the list is a quick nod of accomplishment that she enjoys having throughout her day. It helps her to remain focused on even the smallest things that need her attention. These smaller tasks are generally the tactical, day-to-day activities needed to support her higher-level goals. When she is unable to complete an item, the mere undertaking of moving it from that day to the next can be unsettling enough that it forces her to get it done. If she wants to take this up a notch, she logs it on a family shared calendar on her phone. That means that when she edits the task to be completed the next day, each one of her immediate family members gets a notification that she did not complete the task. Talk about accountability!

Regeanie likes to use a 90-day goal setting process that breaks down bigger visionary goals into quarterly chunks. This process has allowed her to take BHAGs (Big Hairy Audacious Goals) and turn them into something manageable and measurable because they are smaller pieces of the bigger effort. And, because she can experience wins much faster over 90-day cycles versus a year-long goal cycle, it is much more rewarding and motivating. She uses this process with clients and students that she coaches as well.

Another important recommendation that we have when starting to look at goal setting is to become much more specific in identifying your goals. Many people establish goals that are far too vague and broad. Keeping goals vague doesn't help to accomplish them. In fact, it hinders the process by leaving room for backing out of the goal commitment, resulting in incomplete goals. Goals require commitment and discipline, and they also require clarity in order to see the commitment through to completion.

DEFINING THE "WHY" BEHIND YOUR GOAL

Establishing a goal begins with understanding why you are setting it in the first place. Goals should be personal and motivated by something that is important to you. Sometimes, individuals set goals because someone else has told them they should or because they believe that it will make someone else in their life happy. However, when you set a goal because someone else wants the end result, there is less likelihood of achieving the goal or staying motivated to achieve it when things become challenging. Why? Because the goal is not truly yours and, inevitably, you therefore won't stay committed to completing it.

As you begin the goal setting process, make sure that you identify the reason that you want to achieve each goal. Although it's not necessary to have a separate reason for each goal, it is very plausible to have one overarching reason that drives all of your goals. This is often something such as a life mission or purpose statement. Whatever method you choose to use in identifying your reason, make sure that the end reason is strong enough to keep you committed to the goal.

GOAL SETTING THE SMART WAY

Goal setting requires that you are SMART. We are not suggesting that your IQ has to be off the charts, or that you carried a 4.0 GPA while in school. Instead, we are referring to the acronym that is associated with the goal setting process. Let's examine what it really means to be a SMART goal setter.

Natalie always remembers when she learned the importance of goal setting. Years ago, she took on a social media administration role for a group called The AuDLifestyle. This is a group of audiologists who support each other on Facebook and challenge each other to live good lives and stay strong through healthy eating and exercise. One of her good friends, Dr. Amit Gosalia, started the group, and he was adamant about each participant listing out SMART goals. In fact, this process was so critical to being a part of the group that in order to even be accepted into the group, participants were required to complete the exercise. Dr. Gosalia wanted everyone to know that this was a group that was serious about achieving their goals. Through this particular group, Natalie learned to consistently apply the SMART method to the identification of her goals.

SMART stands for Specific, Measurable, Actionable, Realistic, and Timebound. It is a proven method of creating effective goals that, if done correctly, can lead you to achieve everything that you desire.

Setting SMART goals is an iterative process. You will find yourself going over your goals multiple times and making changes as you apply the different components of the SMART process. Give yourself grace, and don't get frustrated. Each time you refine your goals, you will gain a better understanding of them, and they will be planted more deeply, allowing you to truly own them.

Specific

Being clear on the goal helps you to take action on it and actually achieve it. Many people struggle at the onset of setting goals simply because they don't make them specific enough. The more specific the goals, the easier it will be to achieve them. When you have clarity on the goal, it's easier to make decisions because you know exactly what we are trying to achieve.

As you begin to think about your goals, ask yourself a few questions, starting with the most obvious: "What goal do I want to accomplish?" Next, "Why is the goal important to me?" Then, "What do I need in order to accomplish the goal?" Finally, "What obstacles might get in the way of my achieving the goal?"

Measurable

If you can't measure the goal, you can't determine whether or not you've reached it. There must be a clear way of measuring your success in achieving the goal. This helps you to determine if and when the goal is complete and allows measurement of progress both during and after.

If you can't prove to someone else that the goal is

complete, your goal measure is likely

not specific enough. The best test for measurability is to ask yourself, "If someone asked me about my results, can I clearly articulate the way I determined that a goal was accomplished?"

Actionable/Achievable

Your goals must be actionable, which means action can be taken to make them happen. If the path to reaching a goal is completely out of your control, it is not truly actionable, and you will likely fail to complete it.

You will also sometime see this letter in the acronym referred to as Attainable or Achievable. This means that the goal must be something that you actually believe that you can achieve, and that it is reasonable enough for you to have some chance of accomplishing it if you put the right support system in place.

Making the goal action-oriented also encourages you to write active and not passive goals.

Realistic

The goal should be reasonably within your reach. It's important that we feel good about the goals that we set and that we see the possibility of achieving them.

You should ask yourself whether or not it is physically possible for you to complete the goal. If it isn't, you should consider establishing a goal that is more realistic. Consider setting "goal ranges" with a low-end, mid-level, and stretch-level of achievement. This way, if you aim for the low-end of the achievement and see that you can reasonably push yourself beyond it, you can celebrate a significant win by reaching the mid- or stretch-level. When you set unrealistic goals, you are much more likely to lose motivation and abandon them altogether.

This is another letter in the acronym that is sometimes referred to in a different way. Some refer to the "R" as Relevant, which means that the goal must have meaning to you and be relevant to you personally.

Timebound

When you don't attach a date of completion for the goal, you are much less motivated to place focus on it. You have less incentive to work hard and stay diligent in the process. Pick a date that you find inspiring but not overwhelming. You can also consider using date ranges (low-end, target, and stretch).

THE IMPORTANCE OF REVIEWING AND MEASURING YOUR GOALS

Achieving goals requires that you review them regularly, measure your progress, and have the flexibility to make adjustments if necessary. The process of regularly reviewing your goals helps you take greater ownership of your desired results, and more importantly, it allows you to visualize those results on a regular basis. After all, you are 100 percent responsible for your outcomes. Your outcomes are a direct result of your combined thoughts and actions. As such, the actions that you take to accomplish your goals and the thoughts that you use to achieve them are the formula by which you will get to the finish line. Regular review and measurement are vitally important to the overall process.

Regular reviewing of goals is a success habit, and like all good habits, it should be incorporated into a regular routine—preferably a daily or weekly routine. Make sure you have your goals written down on paper or in an electronic journal or planner. Choose the method that you are most likely to use on a regular basis. Look at your goals daily or weekly, and make sure that your day's or week's activities support one or more of them.

Your review process should also incorporate visualization. As you review your goals, try to visualize the outcomes. Consider the answers to the following questions: What will I be doing? Where will I be? How will I feel when I've achieved the goals? Visualization is a powerful practice in achieving your goals because the focus is placed on outcomes, which can have greater impact when it comes to aligning behaviors for success.

The greatest key to successful goal setting is not giving up. Having a vision of what the goal accomplishment will look like can keep you focused and on track. Seeing the end result in your mind is a huge motivator. Even better, have a picture of the anticipated outcome that you can look at every day as a reminder of what you are working towards.

We also wanted to share that during an interview with Dr. Gosalia while we were editing our book, he told us about something that he discovered and has started using in his goal setting process. He found a model that incorporates the review process into the SMART acronym, and he has adopted it into his process. This revised model uses the acronym SMARTER, where the "E" represents evaluation of your goals to help shift patterns to lead to more success and the last "R" represents rewarding yourself once you've accomplished the goal. An award allows you to pause and celebrate your wins—all of you wins—and makes it easier to reset your motivation and start with new goals.

5 Reasons Some People Fail to Achieve Their Goals

Where are you right now in your journey? Are you planning to start something new in your life? Maybe something you might have always wanted to do but have never actually done? Many people remember that they tried and experienced the failure in achieving their goals in the past and are now asking what could have gone wrong. All of those learning experiences shed light on the previous result and lead us to discuss five reasons why goals may not be realized:

Fear of Taking Risks

Risks are everywhere. They are part of business, employment, life, and everyday activities. They may only differ in the degree to which they affect you, but risks are present in everything we do. More importantly, it is imperative to know and understand how to handle and manage them. Risks should never paralyze you, keeping you from moving forward towards achieving your goals.

Too Many Goals

People are often excited to be involved and say yes too often. If you are that type of person, remember: Do things one at a time. Start by first choosing the most important task that you need to accomplish and assign it within a specific and measurable period of time. If you find it difficult to determine where to start or what to prioritize first, it can be helpful to find a coach or consultant who can give you guidance. You may also purchase some self-help books from which you can learn tips and principles on managing goal setting.

Procrastination

You may be surprised to wake up one day and realize that you are wandering more than actually focusing on the steps that will lead you to completion of your goals. If you have tasks and short-term goals that need to be completed, decide to do them right away instead of putting them off. Also, consider why you are procrastinating. Sometimes, procrastination is a symptom of something deeper than simply "putting something off." It could be a symptom of fear or self-sabotage.

Failure to Innovate

Many companies and corporations are forced to shut down because their products are no longer relevant to their market. One reason for this is failure to innovate. At some point, it is critical to your success that you look for ways to advance your business, product, or system. In this modern world, one of the ways to survive and continue achieving your goals is a breakthrough, aha moment, or spontaneous idea that will better your endeavor.

Lack of Motivation

People lose motivation when working toward goals for various reasons. More often than not, however, it's related to a lack of relevance or connectedness to the goal. This is why it's critical that when you define a goal you also determine why the goal is important to you. If you don't have a good reason to achieve the goal, you will lose interest, and worse, you will no longer be committed.

Even if you have been challenged in the past with the goal setting process, don't allow yourself to become frustrated and just stop. Instead, look at scaling back your goals and setting yourself up for greater success. Once you've successfully achieved a few goals, your new goal setting confidence will provide the perfect environment to push yourself to set more goals with greater complexity. Remember, the tortoise didn't win the race because he was the fastest. He won because he was consistently moving forward at a steady pace.

Chapter Review

- Stay motivated by attaching a "why" to your goal. Knowing why you want to achieve the goal in the first place will help keep you motivated to continue, especially when things seem challenging.
- SMART is an acronym that stands for Specific, Measurable, Actionable, Realistic, and Timebound. It is a proven method of creating effective goals.
- Be clear when setting goals, as doing so helps you to take action and actually achieve those goals.

- If you can't prove to someone else that the goal is complete, your goal measurement is likely not specific enough.
- Make your goal action-oriented, which encourages you to write active and not passive goals.

Time to ACT!

Today's Date:

Assess – Journal about what you wish to take action on related to this chapter's topic.

Commit – Write down the action you are willing to commit to in the next twelve months.

Transform – Identify an actionable goal that will transform the commitment into a measurable outcome.

CHAPTER NINE

PARTNERS IN CRIME (ACCOUNTABILITY)

"It is not only what we do, but also what we do not do, for which we are accountable."
—Moliere

NATALIE'S STORY

I have learned a *lot* about accountability in the past eighteen months.

At first, it scared me. I wasn't sure if I would be able to hold up my side of the bargain. I knew it was easy for me to keep up with someone else's goals and continue to challenge them to take steps towards them because I knew I could encourage and keep organized for someone else. That was easy; it pushed the focus off of me. But accountability goes both ways.

The issue for me was wondering, "*Can* I continue to push myself and reach my goals so that I can come back and make sure I stay accountable to my partner?" That is the harder part. Pushing myself and not allowing myself to become stagnant. Asking for advice and help in reaching my goals—and taking that advice rather than ignoring it. I mean, why wouldn't I want that; it would only continue to push me forward! So, I jumped in. I agreed to be accountability partners with Regeanie, and man did it change my life…for the better!

REGEANIE'S STORY

Like Natalie, I have learned a lot over the past year and a half about accountability and trusting someone else other than my husband to help me stay accountable to what I have identified as being important to me. I often joke that I have commitment issues, but truth be told, that isn't entirely untrue. One of my biggest challenges when it comes to commitment is that it's easier to talk myself out of my goals than it is to give someone else excuses as to why I'm not staying on target.

I really didn't relish the idea of giving up this "power." I bet some of you can relate. There is a certain comfort in knowing that if you keep your aspirations to yourself, you don't have to explain it to anyone else if you abandon them. Well, I had to tell myself that that is a lame perspective; it's *exactly* why I need accountability and an accountability partner. Once I moved past this limiting thinking and gave myself a swift kick in the butt, I was able to commit to myself and Natalie to be a good accountability partner who is committed to the process. This was key!

WHY WE NEED ACCOUNTABILITY

There are so many ways to "hide" or think that we are okay living in the status quo. When we only have ourselves to answer to, it's easy to find ways to justify our lack of action with excuses.

"I worked a long day today and deserve a break when I get home." (So you reward yourself with a glass or two of wine. A dessert. A break from working out. Bingeing on TV shows. After all, no one will know.)

"I will do it tomorrow."
"Skipping one day won't hurt."
"I'm really tired, and my body needs a break."
"Having a treat just once is okay."

This approach applies to many things in our lives that we are able to set goals for as well as observe the levels others are reaching through conversation, social media, and the media itself. A fine line is drawn between comparison and inspiration when it comes to the areas in which we hold ourselves accountable, including health, relationships, and business or professional goals.

Now, we are not saying to push yourself until you break, or that you shouldn't relax and indulge yourself every once in a while. We are simply saying that you have to be more committed to your goals than your indulgences, and you must be accountable for your actions. If you don't have accountability associated with your goals, then it becomes too easy to waiver on the commitment.

HOW TO "DO" ACCOUNTABILITY

Accountability can come in different forms. An accountability partner. A Facebook group. A development coach. A mastermind that meets weekly or monthly. The most important aspect of accountability is that there is commitment, and each participant in the accountability partnership agrees to support the completion of the identified goal(s). (Though there are several ways to approach accountability, and we do discuss some of them, you will find that we focus more on accountability partnerships specific to two individuals, similar to the path that we have taken.)

Accountability is critically important in reaching your goals. On the days when you are on fire, an accountability partner celebrates your wins with you. On the days when you are wanting to throw in the towel, an accountability partner pulls you out of the darkness or helps you get unstuck. On the days when you have plenty of energy but may not be motivated, it helps to have that extra "umph" of support, reminding you why you are doing what you are doing.

When you choose an accountability partner who is also looking to stay accountable to his/her goals, it is not only about what that person can do to help you reach your goals but also how you can help them to do the same. Can you provide your ability to just listen on certain days in order to be there for someone else? Are you able to listen with an open mind on behalf of another person in order to offer up ideas to help them pivot and/or get past a block? Are you able to offer suggestions and resources to assist your partner to simply move forward?

Accountability starts with a commitment to better yourself. And, if you have a partner who is in search of the same support, it requires a commitment on your part to give as much as you desire to receive. This bi-directional support-relationship requires a full commitment by both accountability partners. It is almost synonymous to a marriage. Both accountability partners must be open to give and receive, and both must be willing to take the input, assess it, and apply where it makes sense. It is always easy to give out suggestions and ideas for someone else to improve, but it isn't always as easy accept suggestions and make necessary changes yourself, especially if you are not able to see it yet. The one thing you do *not* want to do is constantly ask for suggestions or help, and then not take the suggestions that you receive. Doing so makes it difficult for the person helping you to continue to be there for you going forward.

HOW DO YOU MAKE SURE ACCOUNTABILITY WORKS?

Commitment

Set up a time to make sure you have not scheduled anything else that can get in the way of the sacred time to share where you are in your process. This time should be a standing day and time, not to be rescheduled, and not something that you can skip out on or say, "I will show up next time." This commitment is the key to showing that you are willing to be accountable to yourself and to the other person.

Time

One of the easiest excuses to roll off of a busy entrepreneur's tongue is, "I don't have time." Time is one of the greatest gifts you can give someone else, as well as yourself. Making time can be difficult, but it must be a priority if you want the accountability process to work. This is true even if you are achieving accountability through a group mastermind or group coaching, or you have hired a developmental coach. Many of us are very busy multi-tasking, making lists, and getting things done for multiple people, but committing to carving out time for your self-growth is part of accountability.

Committing to your goals and staying accountable also requires that you stay accountable to yourself. You won't always have the luxury of an accountability partner or group to help you achieve your win. In this case, you must be able to stay committed to the process without assistance. This is when it becomes important to utilize tools like habit reminder apps on your phone, or setting appointments with yourself to regularly do what you've committed to in order to reach your goal.

We both have experienced this in a big way as it relates to our health. While working on the book, we each experienced minor health concerns that caused us to become more intentional about implementing healthier habits. Natalie's focus and commitment started after a professional reviewed her daily schedule to determine how she could implement small changes to support a healthier lifestyle. She was told that since she only had a few minutes in her day to focus on something new, she should think about, and identify, what one thing she was willing to commit to doing during those few valuable minutes. While going through this exercise, she realized that she had multiple options, but she needed to choose an option that aligned with her values, would be enjoyable, and most importantly, that she would be able to stick to. She ultimately chose what she felt she could stick to and would support her goal toward overall health improvement. Not only did this experience teach her the value of making time to implement small changes leading to a goal, it also helped her to better understand how she was spending her time and using her overall busy lifestyle as an excuse not to commit to her goal. This was a vital part of becoming accountable to her goal of leading a healthier lifestyle.

Meeting Frequency

Think about the time it may take you to reach and readily work on a goal established during your most recent accountability meeting. If one or two weeks is too short for a regular meeting interval and doesn't allow enough time to reach action items identified during the previous meeting, you may find yourself frustrated trying to meet an unreasonable timeline. In this case, once a month may be more attainable. However, if setting an aggressive goal pushes you to work harder to reach that goal, meeting every one or two weeks may help. Any longer than a month likely draws it out too long. The real key is choosing the meeting time, being committed to reaching your goals by that meeting, and showing up for the meeting no matter what.

Choose a Person or a Group of People

Accountability can be found in partnering with one other person, as well as with a group. Unlike a mastermind, one-on-one accountability is effective in the sense that you are not able to hide behind someone else. Accountability works best one-on-one when you can show up and share—good or bad—where you are in the journey, how you need help, and it is time to pause and celebrate small wins. Having too big an accountability group can prove difficult for many people. Although you may be accountable, it may be challenging to get around to everyone in each session, and some may be intimated or reluctant to fully disclose in the larger group. Conversations sometimes veer off topic—and don't come back! Setting yourself up for both getting the work done *and* success requires accountability with fewer participants who may branch off of a mastermind group. On the other hand, accountability in a group setting *can* effectively help with some areas of the journey. When you are not ready to act on an idea but are continuing to learn from others along the journey, showing up in a group can keep you grounded, inspired, and motivated.

Set Goals

Always have a short list of goals to work on before your next meeting, and make sure you are able to touch upon each goal during the meeting. Touching on it may mean revealing that you've completed the goal or are still working on it, and have become stuck, not knowing what the next step may be. As long as you talk about where you are with each goal you've set, it helps you in staying accountable, no matter where you are in the process.

Be Sure to Give and *Take*

It is important to make sure that not only do you help others and share in their process, but that you are able to allow for help toward your process. As accountability partners, make sure to spend time discussing *both* of your journeys. Also understand that if one journey needs more help than the other at a particular point in time, it is alright to spend some extra time helping your partner maneuver through the thought process. But, be mindful of both taking more time to discuss the needs of the other person *and* not allowing time for the other person to be on the "hot seat." Otherwise, you could find that the meeting only focuses on one person's journey and goals, leaving the other person with no support when the meeting is over. If this does happen, make sure that it is agreed by both partners prior to the meeting start, and commit to make the next meeting devoted to the partner who was not the focus. Also, make sure that this type of one-sided accountability meeting is the exception and not the norm.

Find the Right Person

It is extremely important to find the *right* person to partner with for accountability. It should be someone who is like-minded as it relates to being goal-oriented and having a strong desire to get things done. Keep in mind that your accountability partner should be in a place where they are committed to taking action. This person should support you in your dreams and encourage your pursuits but also be willing to point out possible flaws in your plans and help you to identify solutions to address the flaws. It should be someone who pushes you, asks questions, and adds value to your partnership. If you start to notice that it's not a good fit, it is okay to respectfully end the arrangement and find someone else who is a better fit.

In addition to having a primary accountability partner, we can't stress enough the importance of having the *right* people in your life to encourage you to ignite the power that you have within. One of our friends and colleagues, Cherie Mathews has always encouraged Natalie to do more because she always saw more in her. Cherie is the Founder and CEO of Heal In Comfort (healincomfort.com), a postoperative shirt for those recovering from mastectomy surgery. Cherie is an inventor, owns patents for her products, is an amazing entrepreneur and philanthropist, and she is a breast cancer survivor. She has always pushed Natalie to go after more and to look at incorporating key concepts such as multiple streams of income into her overall life and business strategy. Cherie is another amazing friend and mentor that we have both learned from because of what she models in her own personal and professional life. We feel truly blessed to have individuals like Cherie who pour into us personally to make us better and to help us actualize the power that we have within. We know that this is a critical component to our ability to continuously take action in our lives.

Has this made you think about who has been this person in your life? Maybe you can be this person in someone else's life? Take that first action step and reach out!

Chapter Review

- Accountability can come in different forms. The most important aspects of accountability are commitment and mutual benefit.
- Accountability requires a commitment of time. Time is one of the greatest gifts you can give someone else, as well as yourself.
- Choose a meeting time, be committed, take the time to complete the action items and milestones that you've agreed to, and most importantly, show up, even if you have to apologize because you didn't complete all that you agreed to.
- One-on-one accountability is effective because you are not able to hide behind the efforts of the group and time spent discussing the accomplishments of others.
- Group accountability can be helpful for different stages of the journey, especially if you are

at the start of the goal setting process and you are looking to learn from others who can keep you grounded, inspired, and motivated.
- Always have a short list of goals to work on before your accountability meetings, and make sure you are able to provide status on each goal during the meeting.
- It is important to find the right accountability partner who is like-minded, supportive, honest, respectful of your time and your dreams, and who can challenge you to reach your personal best.

Time to ACT!

Today's Date:

Assess – Journal about what you wish to take action on related to this chapter's topic.

Commit – Write down the action you are willing to commit to in the next twelve months.

Transform – Identify an actionable goal that will transform the commitment into a measurable outcome.

CHAPTER TEN

TAKE ME TO YOUR MASTER...MIND (MASTERMINDS)

"It's said that a wise person learns from his mistakes. A wiser one learns from others' mistakes. But the wisest person of all learns from others' successes."
—John C. Maxwell

No one has all of the answers or knows everything. We all get "stuck" at times and do not know what the next step is or who we need to reach out to next. If you are working alone, this can be dangerous—you can find yourself unable to get to the next step for a very long time! So long, sometimes, that you may never move forward.

One choice is to reach out to friends and other professionals and ask them a question. Beware that this approach can prove a bit dangerous for a few reasons:

It could be one-sided. You may reach out to someone who is consistently helping you, which can be exhausting and unfair to the other party.

You end up with "too many cooks in the kitchen," and have too many choices, making you even more confused.

You pick the wrong person to open up to and share your ideas or where you might be stuck, and end up with the idea not moving forward because you are talked out of it, they give you a strong opinion against it and you care about their opinion, or you decide that holding back may be the "safe" option.

Getting involved in a mastermind scared us at first. The word itself seemed like an over-the-top, overused way for people to get together. We wondered whether we would get much out of it, or worse, may not have anything of value to offer someone else! But as we learned more about what a mastermind truly is, it became exciting to know that we were going to have some accountability to make sure our ideas and businesses grew.

WHAT IS A MASTERMIND?

Even though I (Natalie) wanted to be a part of a mastermind and knew it would and could help me, I still didn't fully understand what it was. When both Regeanie's and my "word of the year" turned out to be ACTION, Regeanie almost immediately suggested joining a mastermind. It sounded like a good idea, so I walked into the unknown and learned along the way. The biggest thing I learned about a mastermind was that it really should consist of two things: a small conglomerate of people who have both gone before you and will follow in your footsteps so that you can give and take; and, each person should be able to provide support and suggestions as well as connections for resources to help people grow in their businesses. Please note that while business owners and entrepreneurs often seek mastermind groups to help move their business goals forward, it is also used by individuals who simply want to be part of a group that is interested in moving similar personal goals forward and holding each other accountable in the process.

NAPOLEON HILL'S DEFINITION OF A MASTERMIND

An individual mastermind is a peer-to-peer mentoring concept in which members help each other solve their problems with input and advice. The concept was coined in 1925 by Napoleon Hill in his book, The Law of Success, and was described in more detail in his 1937 book, Think and Grow Rich. As he stated, a mastermind is "a friendly alliance with one or more persons who will encourage one to follow through with both plan and purpose."

A business mastermind, on the other hand, is a group of business professionals who commit to come together and help each other stay accountable to their business goals.

Although Napoleon Hill called it a "master mind alliance," the concept has since been shortened and modernized to "mastermind group." Mastermind groups are not an uncommon idea, and they have actually been around for many years. Even Benjamin Franklin belonged to a mastermind, which he called a Junto. However, it was Napoleon Hill who was able to explain the concept clearly and encourage people to gather together to assist in the success of each other in a structured and repeatable environment for the success of all. Napoleon Hill wrote about the mastermind group concept as:

"The coordination of knowledge and effort of two or more people, who work toward a definite purpose, in the spirit of harmony." He continued, "No two minds ever come together without thereby creating a third, invisible intangible force, which may be likened to a third mind [the master mind]."

MASTERMIND ALLIANCES

Masterminds are a combination of brainstorming, education, peer-to-peer accountability, and support in a group setting intended to sharpen one's business and personal skills. A mastermind group is designed to help both you and your mastermind group members achieve success. Members are expected to challenge each other to set strong goals—and accomplish them.

Mastermind group facilitators are expected to start the groups, run them, and keep discussions on time and topic. They guide the group to go deep into discussions and work with members to create success as each member defines it for himself or herself. Facilitators are the hidden gem in thriving mastermind groups. Many groups fail because of poor leadership.

Through a mastermind group process, a goal is created, followed by a plan designed to achieve that goal. The group may help with creative ideas and decision making. As you begin to implement your plan, the subsequent group meetings allow you to present to the group both success stories and problems. Success stories are applauded and celebrated, while problems are dissected and solved through peer brainstorming along with collective and creative thinking.

The group requires commitment and confidentiality along with a willingness to give and receive advice and a willingness to support each other with total honesty, respect, and compassion. Mastermind group members play many roles, as they are catalysts for growth, devil's advocates, and supportive colleagues. This is the true essence and value of a strong mastermind group.

Let's pause to talk again about commitment. Commitment is critical in a mastermind or any other form of accountability. Commitment is a mindset, and continuing to commit—even when you don't feel like it—is crucial to the process. The act of continuing to move forward becomes easier as your brain starts recognizing a particular rhythm or pattern in your decision-making. Your brain is able to decipher patterns, and ultimately, remember them. Even if it isn't yet able to decipher them, it remembers them. This helps in any form of retraining of the brain, as memories and lessons learned—whether good or bad—help you make future decisions more quickly. As decisions and patterns are formed and repeated, the commitment you have in the forefront of your brain can lead to habituation and even desensitization of certain patterns.

The reason I know this is that, as an audiologist, I work with patients who are hypersensitive – sometime to patterns they have recognized, such as certain sounds—even moderate, everyday sounds. Sounds start their pathway at the level of the ear, but then goes to the sub-cortical level of the brain where we are able to detect things. If the received sounds have no meaning, they go "out the door," and we pay no further attention to it. But, when certain sounds begin to be present more often, the awareness allows our brain to continually focus on it. Sounds then rise to the cortical level of our brain, where we don't just detect it but also perceive it and evaluate it. Once that happens, sounds can start to have meaning – maybe as a pattern, or maybe as sounds with emotional attachment, meaning that it is now in the limbic system and can linger.

Further on from the limbic system, if we start to have physiological manifestations because of a particular sound, it begins to engage the autonomic nervous system. This is how sound delivers a person from "hearing" to "listening" and to "connecting" to a sound or patterns of sounds. In order to reduce the detection and lingering of certain patterns, I use sound therapy to reduce the signal-to-noise ratio of a patterned sound in order to help facilitate habituation.

The same process holds true in terms of the way we recognize or detect a pattern in our personal or professional pursuits. What's important to identify is whether or not the pattern will be distracting and detract our attention from what we need to focus on. Or, like sound therapy, will the pattern actually help us decrease the "noise" so much that we are able to further tune out the pattern and continue to stay focused? Although masterminds can be very helpful and are made up of people who are expected to give you feedback and ideas to move forward, it's important to assess whether or not such a group will be "too noisy," creating distraction, or are there ways it can help you focus and stay the course?

Mastermind meetings work best when there is an agenda for the group to follow and the conversations stay on topic. The group facilitator is tasked with making sure that conversations are balanced, helpful, and supportive as well as that group meeting agenda items are covered in the time period allotted.

In a mastermind group, the agenda is created by and belongs to the group, and participation and commitment are key. Mastermind partners give feedback, brainstorm new possibilities, and set up accountability structures that will help keep one's focus strong. The group becomes a community of supportive colleagues who brainstorm together in order to move the members to new levels. A large advantage of a mastermind group is the tremendous insights gained, which improve both your business and personal life. A member of a mastermind group should always seek to create massive value for everyone in the group. It is like having an objective board of directors, a success team, and a peer advisory group all rolled into one.

Our first mastermind in which we participated was held just between the two of us. We started out with an accountability call to be able to hear what each other was working on and offer ideas or otherwise help take each other to the next step.

The next mastermind in which we participated was a group of women all working on making our businesses and projects into something bigger. We gathered different minds together to make a collective team. Although we were all friends, we started the group by implementing a non-disclosure agreement. Next, we wanted to make sure each person had enough time to share and discuss their needs to move to the next step. We decided on a meeting day and time, frequency, and decided to rotate facilitators/moderators to keep us on time. Lastly, we included the opportunity to share things in both our personal lives and our business lives that we may need advice, guidance, or help on. We would meet every two weeks and share the greatest challenge we would face in the following two weeks. Once a challenge was shared, we offered ideas, contacts, and next steps. We also threw out challenges to complete over the next two weeks. We celebrated wins, and we shared opportunities.

Other Things to Consider when Forming a Mastermind

Consider the Size of the Mastermind Group

If the group is too small, it may not be effective. If it's too large, it can be difficult to focus on the people who need to be focused on, and there may be too many ideas and suggestions to help a specific person. Six to eight people is a great place to start. Consider staying with an even number of people, as it allows pairing off to form smaller groups if needed.

Implement Formalities

Consider the use of a non-disclosure form, commitment form, and mastermind rules. These are all intended to help facilitate a useful and supportive environment. Masterminds involve showing up for each other and participating as a sounding board, a challenger, an accountability partner, and an encourager. It requires commitment, understanding, and the ability to step back to see suggestions from a new, and possibly different, perspective. It requires selflessly giving ideas, connections, and resources to help someone else in their journey. It also requires diligence to complete goals prior to the next mastermind gathering.

Are you looking for a mastermind group? Maybe this has sparked your excitement to be part of a mastermind group? Or lead one yourself? Stay tuned as we have some incredible plans to help people mastermind and to be able to both help others and learn from others as they grow and build their success stories. Get connected to us!

Chapter Review

- An individual mastermind group is a peer-to-peer mentoring concept in which members help each other solve their problems with input and advice from other members.
- A business mastermind is a group of business professionals who commit to come together and help each other stay accountable to their business goals.
- Mastermind groups require commitment, confidentiality, and willingness to both give and receive advice and ideas.

- Mastermind groups support each other with total honesty, respect, and compassion.
- Mastermind group members may act as catalysts for growth, devil's advocates, and supportive colleagues.

Time to ACT!

Today's Date:

Assess – Journal about what you wish to take action on related to this chapter's topic.

Commit – Write down the action you are willing to commit to in the next twelve months.

Transform – Identify an actionable goal that will transform the commitment into a measurable outcome.

CHAPTER ELEVEN

HEALTHY CHOICES LEAD TO A HEALTHY YOU (BOUNDARIES)

"No is a complete sentence."

We've all accepted tasks, jobs, maybe even relationships that have turned out not to be healthy decisions. But how long did we stay or let things remain status quo? How long did we hope that things would change and get better? I (Natalie) have learned about setting, managing, and maintaining healthy boundaries through some difficult lessons. Oddly enough, most have been in the last five years of my professional life.

My first lesson was through a betrayal.

There is a term often used in basketball, "wolf," which refers to a moment someone has taken the ball down the court on a fast break, and someone else comes up from behind to try to steal the ball away. I was very good friends with a woman whom I trusted and looked up to for about five years, I felt blessed by our relationship, as it began with respect and collaboration. There was no jealousy; no comparison; just openness, honesty, and helping each other build and grow in our business. Over time, the dynamic changed. Activities I spent my time on in order to build my connections became difficult to share. Comments such as "You need to include me." and "That isn't fair!" started to surface. Then came the berating behind closed doors of which I spoke in an earlier chapter.

I should have walked away the first time it happened, but I didn't because I received a heartfelt apology and promise that it would never happen again. I believed and hoped that her words came from a place of true authenticity—something that exists in a "real" woman-to-woman friendship when there is mutual respect and support for one another. I quickly came to learn that this was not the case for this particular friendship. Then, it happened again, and again, and yet again. After a great deal of hurt, though reluctant, I chose to close the door to this relationship because I realized that it was toxic. It was not a healthy environment for me, and it turned me into a different person, one who hid, who didn't believe in herself, and who was very angry. I was so angry, in fact, that I could no longer focus on becoming who I needed to be in order to impact the world, and that angered me even more. What I did learn from this experience was the importance of being cognizant and aware of signs of negativity and never allowing it to stall me ever again.

Have your plans or successes ever been thwarted because someone was undermining you or executing a sneak attack from behind in order to take you down? Was it someone you trusted? Did betrayal come into play? Rather than blame other people for being negative—you know, those nay-sayers or trolls that enter our lives—we must instead focus on how to establish healthy boundaries so that we can continue to TAKE ACTION in spite of their malicious activities. It is critical to recognize when boundaries are needed and when it is time to remove people from our lives. This may be very difficult to do if we feel an attachment or obligation, or if it is a family member. However, knowing when to say, "Enough is enough!" and respectively exiting from the relationship is a skill that is needed to ensure that those who disguise themselves as supporters (but really aren't) do not continue to derail your efforts to move forward.

My next lesson came through an "energy drain" (I also like to use the term "energy vampire"). I was hired to use my energy, ideas, professional expertise, and stature to help a company make connections to clients and add an educational component to their already developed sales team. I worked well and hard in this environment for many months, until I felt my energy start to deplete from repetitive "coaching" on ways that I could improve, while the internal team cohesiveness crumbled. Trying to read the early signs of negativity surrounding the company, both internally and from outside feedback while also attempting to preserve my energy, I tried to exit the relationship after six months.

Unfortunately, I allowed myself to be talked into another six months on the job. I thought that it would work since I negotiated specific hours that I would be available to focus my energy. As I persevered through the commitment, giving everything I had, I continued to be mentally, emotionally, and professionally depleted. I finally permanently ended the commitment and decided that it was more important to stay true to what was important to me than to feel the burden of an unwarranted obligation. I felt as though a weight had been lifted from my shoulders. I also learned another valuable lesson: You should never allow someone else to "talk" you into accepting a commitment if you are not fully aligned with it.

When examining healthy boundaries, we have to consider our own time and energy, and be knowledgeable about how to protect both. It is also very important to understand your personal values and what is important to you. When your decisions and actions are grounded in your core values, it is much more difficult to allow others to overstep the boundaries that you have identified.

Time is a predictor of what you choose and what you believe is important to you. These are personal decisions, and it shouldn't matter what people think of the way you spend your time. We must be cognizant of ways to protect and maintain the time that belongs to us and when we are choosing to give it away. With regard to time:

- Take a break when you can; even a short break can re-energize you.
- Spend time doing things you believe in—the relationship you want to build, the tasks that will help you grow and succeed in your personal life and business.
- Practice saying no to things you don't need to say yes to - ask yourself, "Can someone else do this?"
- Figure out sensical ways to reorganize your time (i.e., waking up earlier, even though the tradeoff may be getting to bed earlier; if you say yes to something, be sure to say no to something else in order to make room for the task you said yes to).
- Define your values and be VERY clear on them.
- In order to be successful, you also have to know things about your energy specifically,

and where you are choosing to place it.

What fuels your energy? When do you need to be re-fueled? How do you get there? For us, sometimes it is rest, other times it is connecting with people—sometimes like-minded people, sometimes hearing about others' success or what they are working on, or helping them get to the next level

Consider what you can give and take to maintain your energy. If you decide to wake up early to work out or to tune in to three or four shows before work, you may have to give up time at night to get your work done and go to bed early. You can't keep running and running. People often say, "I'll sleep when I sleep," but that isn't true. We end up collapsing. It quickly becomes evident that in order to put our best foot forward, we must take care of ourselves and be intentional about where we place our energy.

A final lesson I (Natalie) learned about my own energy was through an unhealthy repetitive cycle. This one was hard because I believed in the mission of what I was involved in. I was in for a total of three years. Each year, the things that the organization promised to do aligned with what was important to me, and this made me feel that I would be helping to make a difference. I watched as the promises, a hope-filled vision, and various connections were being made to support the communicated goals. I worked hard to gather the right people to rally behind the cause. However, year after year, the promises never came to fruition, and more and more of my professional acquaintances stopped participating. I stayed positive in the belief that the next year would be better, with a new team and fresh ideas, and I worked hard again. Still, I watched as people were let down and became even more disconnected. How I wished I could have stayed longer to finally witness a win for this group, but to my knowledge, the hopeful vision still hasn't manifested. This experience made me feel like a hamster running on a wheel, not knowing when to get off. Finally, I did make the decision; I simply had to jump off of the hamster wheel.

Having healthy boundaries means practicing when to say yes and when to say no. I can't imagine saying "yes" to everything, yet we've heard of people successfully doing this as part of their growth journey. Television writer, producer, and author Shonda Rhimes wrote and released her first book in 2016, titled Year of Yes: How to Dance It Out, Stand In the Sun, and Be Your Own Person. Though she was the creator of highly successful TV shows such as "Grey's Anatomy" and "Scandal", she suffered from debilitating social anxiety and shame associated with her weight. She talks about the total life change that she experienced when she committed to saying "yes" for an entire year.

I once sat down with a councilwoman who shared with me her journey of a similar commitment to saying "yes" to everything for an entire year. I was shocked. If challenged, would you agree to do this?

Saying yes definitely opens a door for something new to happen, and it can become a habit as more opportunities are presented. You gain more confidence in being able to ask for more as well as understanding that failure is part of the process. But, saying "yes" can come with a significant draw on your time. You will be faced with so many options that you will have to determine when is the right time to say "no." Just remember that it is healthy to say "no" when the opportunities don't align with your values and what you've determined to be important for you.

**When you say no,
independence, confidence, and relationships grow!**

Eventually, there comes a time when we all have to stand up for ourselves in order to create healthy boundaries. Have you ever felt as though you can't help but say yes…even when you don't want to? Do you find it difficult to say no? Do you find yourself saying yes when you would much rather say no? If so, it's not surprising, as most of us are taught that saying no is selfish. Women, in particular, are socialized to be compliant and selfless. In the workplace, volunteering for tasks or working late is seen as being a good team player. Friends and family might expect you to take responsibility for making them happy or making their lives easier. And, be honest, being "the good person" they can always rely on, who won't let them down—that can feel pretty good, can't it?

But, downgrading your own needs can come at a personal cost. Once you become known as the go-to person who'll always step in to work weekends or take the kids or host Thanksgiving, it can be hard to walk away or share any roles. Saying yes all the time, or even most of the time, often means that:

- you're signaling to the world (and yourself) that your own needs don't matter.
- people expect you to be there all the time to pick up their slack.
- your self-worth depends on other people's approval.
- your boundaries aren't respected and may even become non-existent.
- you will feel increasingly resentful, overburdened, and stressed.
- your relationships won't be based on mutual respect.
- you won't have time for the things you truly want to do!

Rather than thinking of no as negative, realize the positive energy that's packed into this two-letter word. Saying no is powerful, and it will change the way you think about your life – and yourself. Know when to say no—and how to say it in such a way to keep your relationships intact. Be comfortable saying no in a way that you can continue to comfortable do for the rest of your life.

THE POWER OF NO

Most of us are taught from the time we're young to avoid the word no. We use the word to refuse things, turn down opportunities, and declare ourselves unyielding and unmoving.

Early on, we learn beliefs such as:

- "Yes" is bold and energizing, and it makes you open to possibility and opportunity.
- "No" is a slammed door in a locked house.
- "Yes" is the open skies and the wide-open spaces of the world at your disposal.
- "Yes" means you're amenable; it makes us likable. It is welcoming and comfortable.
- "No" represents the greedy friend who will never share. It turns us away.

To be honest, these belief patters paint a pretty grim picture. The sad thing is, most of us go through life never realizing that what we've been taught is wrong.

NO IS REALLY ONLY A BOUNDARY LINE

"No" defines the edges between us and the world. It protects us and makes us stronger. It is the word that holds control of our destiny. With it, you set the standard both for how you wish to be treated and how much you will allow others to dictate your life. The word represents our possibility and opportunity for growth as well as the way that we get things done.

The biggest reason to use the word no is the time wasted when you don't. We all only get twenty-four hours in a day, and it's up to us how we use them. By saying yes to every request, the resulting problem becomes apparent immediately: you run out of time. Your schedule gets so packed that it can feel like it's impossible to breathe, much less get any of your work accomplished. Saying no puts your day back into your own hands. This isn't about being selfish. It's about being protective of one of your most valuable resources. That's not to say you can't spare an hour for a friend or take on that extra project, but you should be the one to decide whether or not doing so is a valuable use of your day.

How do you go about doing that? You start with an understanding of where your hours go and how you spend (or intend to spend) your time. Some people start by writing down everything they are doing during each hour of the day in order to be able to assess how their time is being used. Another approach is to begin by creating a to-do list the night before. This establishes the way you wish to use your time for the day before you even wake up. It's much easier to protect a schedule that's already in place than it is to try to guess how much time you have for extra requests. From there, it's a matter of protecting your time. Be aware of the hours in your day when you're being asked to do something. If you're not sure whether or not you actually do have time to take on something new, there is nothing wrong with asking for some time to consider the request. Doing so gives you an opportunity to check your schedule and see whether you can create time to complete the request.

THE POWER OF YES

When you say yes to everything, anything goes. Being so open to accepting requests ensures that people know they can ask you for the moon, the sun, and half a dozen stars. As it becomes apparent that you're the type to consistently say yes, exploitation of the worst kind is invited into your world. Someone who always says yes is easy to take advantage of. Sadly, human nature dictates that this kind of weakness will be rooted out and used relentlessly by those who are not as kind or as ethical as others. Most of us won't even realize that it's happening to us until it's too late.

How do you know when you're being taken advantage of? Check your feelings. If you're feeling resentful, it's usually a pretty good indicator that you're not being appreciated for your work. Also, be alert for repeat offenders—those who come at you time and time again with requests, one after another.

SAY NO TO ALLOW YOU TO SAY YES

As mentioned before, there truly is only so much we can each do in a day, and therefore, we must be in control of what we do and why. We should be able to pick and choose the things that matter the most to us. How do we do that? Start with a clear understanding of what you hope to gain out of life. What are your goals? Where do you want to be in a year? In three years? In five or ten years? Use those ideas as a template for the things you say yes to.

If an opportunity doesn't align with your core values or serves your purpose, if it doesn't help you to reach your goal or satisfy you in some other way, it's up to you to say no so that when the next beneficial opportunity comes along, you can say yes. It really is just that easy.

Do all of your goals have to be career-oriented? Not at all. We have personal goals as well. Maybe you realize that in five years your kids will be going off to college. That might mean that your goal right now is to spend quality time with them before they go. Saying no to frivolous requests might give you more time for family activities.

Also, when evaluating the things that matter, keep in mind what gets you excited. What captures your interest? If you have a fascination for local politics, a love of books, or a desire to save the whales, you need to figure that into your plans as well. Saying no might create the opportunity to start a book club. Or a petition. Or even to run for local office. None of this would be possible if you'd already overbooked yourself by saying yes to pointless busy work and events.

Saying no frees us up to save our resources, our time, and our energy for those things that we want to do most. This puts the power squarely in our hands, and we once again become the master of our fate. In the end, saying no represents you at your most powerful. Only someone who is confident, healthy, and capable can say no in order to organize their life in the most beneficial ways for themselves. Choose how you spend your time. Then, decide who you want to spend it with. By taking control of your desires, your needs, and your health, you are using no to create a version of you that's the very best.

WHEN TO SAY NO

Knowing that no is powerful and knowing when to use it are often two very different things. It's now time to put it into practice. This is often easier said than done. You can't confidently say no until you understand when it's most advantageous to do so. Let's face it; you can't just say no to everything. If you do that, you will actually stunt your ability to grow and change. Besides, some things you will want to do, while you'll need to do others because of commitments to your job, your family, and/or your friends. This means carefully choosing when you say no so that you're using the tool to your best advantage.

Below, we have complied a list of times to say no to use as a reference. While this doesn't include every possible situation, it does give you a guide that will prove useful as you start to take back the power and control of your own life. While some of these items might seem self-explanatory, let's discuss them each in more detail just to be sure. This list will hopefully help clear up any lingering confusion about just when to say no.

When Something Isn't Your Responsibility

It's all too easy to fall into the trap of riding to the rescue, especially when you're hoping to prove yourself at work or in a certain relationship. The problem is, not everything you're saying yes to is your responsibility. Quite often, you shouldn't be the one to jump in and get involved. When asked to do something, the first thing you have to do is ask yourself whether or not you're the right person for the job. Someone else might be better for the job. More than likely, it was their job to do it in the first place!

When You Are Already Too Busy

Benjamin Franklin said, "If you want something done, give it to a busy person." While this holds a grain of truth, if you're already swamped with things to do, chances are you don't need anything else on your plate. The best way to figure out whether you're too busy is to take a hard look at your schedule. Do you have the room for one more thing? Producing the correct answer will involve brutal honesty. Ask yourself just how long the request is going to take, and figure out how that vibes with your current schedule. Don't underestimate! We tend not to allow ourselves enough time to do things, so we might be already overworked and not even know it.

When It's a Negative Drain on Your Resources

Too often we forget that we only have twenty-four hours a day, and a good number of those need to be spent sleeping. Evaluate your resources right now. How many hours a day do you dedicate to work? What about to family or friends? What about downtime for yourself? When you're asked to take on something new, it's easy to forget that you'll have to take away resources from somewhere else. Can you afford to do so? For example, if you determine that you're considering giving up an hour of sleep or might be skipping a meal in order to take on something new, you're in the danger zone. Taking away from resources necessary to your health and happiness is never a good idea. Neither is giving up time in a day to do something that's going to leave you exhausted. Anytime you say yes to something that leaves a negative impact on your life, it's a bad idea.

When It Isn't Important to You

What someone else perceives as absolutely crucial might not be all that important to you. For example, getting involved in someone's political campaign when you're not invested in a particular candidate is almost never going to go well. If you're trying to do something that you're not emotionally invested in, it's nearly impossible to put forth your best effort. What's more, by taking on the job you might be taking away an opportunity from someone who is passionate about the cause. The solution? Say no whenever you're being asked to jump into something you don't care about.

When You Feel Like You Are Being Taken Advantage Of

The problem with having said "yes" so many times in the past is that now everyone expects a yes when they come to you. Unfortunately, this tends to encourage a certain kind of person to take advantage of the situation – which they do, as often as possible. How can you tell if someone is taking advantage of you? Trust your gut feelings in the situation. If someone is asking something of you, and you immediately feel repulsed, upset, or resentful of the offer, chances are high that the person is taking advantage of you. This is the time you need to learn to trust your instincts. Anytime you feel taken advantage of by a request, say no. This is your cue to get out of the situation before it's too late.

When It's Something That Makes You Uncomfortable

This relates to the previous point, but with a slightly different take. Not every situation that makes you uncomfortable involves someone taking advantage of you. Some requests are just creepy or feel wrong. Again, trust your instincts. If something feels "off," it usually is. As with the last example, say no.

When It's Something that Goes Against Your Core Values

You've been passionate about the environment for a long time, but now someone comes to you and wants you to be part of a political campaign for a candidate who has proven that they don't care about the environment at all. In a situation like that, it's easy to see that you're being asked to do something that goes against your beliefs. But, not every situation is this cut and dried. Before you can determine whether or not a request compromises your beliefs, you need to know what you stand for. You can accomplish this by defining your values and sticking to them. If you're not sure whether something you're being asked to do necessitates a moral compromise, ask for more information. If you are still unclear, ask for some time to think it over so you can research that question for yourself. If it turns out to be something on the wrong side of the fence from your belief system, it's time to say no.

When it Hurts Someone You Care About

This one should go without saying. Anytime you're asked to do something that in any way hurts someone you love, it's time to say no. Nothing is worth the betrayal and hurt that friend or loved one will experience when they find out about your involvement – and they will find out.

When to say no doesn't have to be complicated. Just remember not to overthink things. Most of "saying no" is about having clear boundaries and making sure that no one crosses them without your permission. Where do we go from here? With a pretty clear idea in your head about when and where you want to use the power of no, it's time to learn **exactly how to do it.**

HOW TO SAY NO

The how is the hardest part of the whole concept. Most people aren't comfortable saying the actual word. If you struggle to say no, it likely comes down to one of three reasons:

1. You're afraid of looking bad.
2. You don't like letting people down.
3. You hate conflict.

Saying no becomes a whole lot easier when you realize that people aren't thinking about you as much as you think. That might seem a little harsh, but keep reading; it's not as bad as it sounds. Most people who ask for something are expecting a no even though they're hoping for a yes. More often than not, once they hear no, they move to the next person on their list. You don't look bad. You haven't let anyone down. And, unless you're dealing with a particular kind of individual, there's no need to expect any conflict at all. Even in the worst-case scenario, any conflict that does arise will be minimal. That said, knowing this doesn't lessen the anxiety. This is why knowing how to say no can go a long way toward making this process a whole lot easier. Here are some quick methods that have been proven to work very well when it comes time to say no.

Give Yourself Permission

The first thing to do is permit yourself to intentionally say no. If you've spent your life being nice, this may not be easy. Try writing down all the things you would like to do this week or this month—everything you want to accomplish, from getting to the gym to having a weekend with no commitments to completing a project. Set these as priorities and allow time for them in your schedule. Any extra requests need to fit around your priorities. It's easier to say no and mean it if you've permitted yourself to refuse requests that get in the way of achieving your goals.

Be Quick

If what you're being asked to do is something that you immediately know you don't want any part of, there's no reason to make anyone wait for an answer. Just say no quickly and be done with it. That doesn't mean you shouldn't be polite about it, but there's no need to make endless excuses either. Just a simple "No, thank you" will suffice. How to handle it if they press for more details depends on your audience, but even that should be kept simple. "I'm busy that day" or "I have too much to do" is all the explanation they need.

Be Honest

The worst thing you can do for all involved is come up with an elaborate excuse. For one thing, lies are almost always found out. For another, keeping your lies straight just gives you something else to worry about. Just be honest – but not brutally honest. Saying, "No, I won't go because quite honestly I don't like you" might be a little too much. Instead, saying, "No, I can't go, but thank you for asking" is sufficient. You don't need to say anything else. Less is more.

Be Polite

There's a bit of a myth that saying no is rude and

selfish. The art of saying no can often lie in the delivery. You can say no politely and respectfully, and in a way that makes the other person feel better, not diminished or rejected. If you're still feeling a bit uncertain or even badly about saying no, try the "saying no sandwich" technique, which neatly wraps your refusal between two layers of niceness.

Perhaps you are invited to a dinner party with friends, and you either don't want to go or can't fit it into your schedule. Try this no sandwich response: "Thank you for the invitation, I appreciate it. We always enjoy your cooking (positive). Unfortunately, we can't make it this Saturday (firm, unequivocal no). It would have been lovely to see you; perhaps we can catch up another time (positive with an opening to make an alternative arrangement, if you want to leave that door open). Notice that you don't need to provide a detailed excuse. Saying no just because the offer doesn't suit you is fine.

Be Consistent

Once you've said no, don't allow space for the other person to try to persuade you otherwise. Ignore any emotional blackmail or persistent, repeated request once you've refused. Don't feel guilty or apologize for saying no. In doing so, you're only handing the other person a stick to beat you with in the hope that you'll change your mind! Ignore the "just this once," "pretty please" or other attempts to take advantage of your good nature. If you want people to respect your decisions, you have to stand firm and be polite. Consistency also works well with children and animals. Say no and mean no, and everyone's life will be easier.

Be Prepared

If you feel susceptible to being leaned on to change your mind, arm yourself with a ready-made script, so you feel more confident. It's okay to say, "No, I can't," but if you've been in the position where you already feel like a doormat, you might need some more support. If you're constantly asked to stay late in the office or work weekends or drive the whole neighborhood's kids to sporting events, having a script at-the-ready is a great way to help you stand your ground. Take some time to imagine the scenario in which you refuse. Think of all the things people will try to get you to change your mind, and then come up with a straightforward response to each one. You may not need them, but it's good to have a back-up.

Ask for More Time

Sometimes you know you want to say no, but you can't put into words exactly why that is. This is the ideal moment to say, "I'd like to sleep on that" or something similar, allowing you time to delve a little deeper. Maybe you need to check your schedule or do a little more research. Do what you need to do to figure out why you're saying no. A few things to keep in mind: don't take too long to decide, as that's impolite and even wishy-washy. When you finally do say no, again, keep it simple. There's no need to go back over your long decision-making process. The time taken was to satisfy you—not them.

Reframe

Before you respond to a request, think about whether or not you want to do it, whether it's possible given your current obligations, and what the opportunity cost is. After all, you know you can't do everything. Ask yourself these questions:

- "If I say yes to this, what am I giving up?"
- "What will I not be able to do if I say yes to this?"
- "If I choose to say yes, how will it impact my priorities?"
- "What will saying yes mean in the long-term?"
- "Is saying yes to this request the best use of my time right now?"

Whether you say yes or no, you should carefully consider your response. It's okay not to respond straightaway with a reflex answer. Not only that, taking your time signals to the asker that you're taking their request seriously, and they'll be more likely to respect your decision. And, remember, saying no means being able to say yes to something else.

Suggest an Alternative

If you're feeling especially bad about saying no—it might be the request was something you wanted to do but didn't have room for on your schedule—help the asker identify an alternative. It's fine to offer alternate options, but only if you feel comfortable. Don't let it become another stick to get you to change your mind. For example, you might offer to do it later, when you have time in your schedule. If it turns out that there is a deadline on this offer, and the requester truly can't wait for you, maybe you could suggest someone else who might be the perfect fit for the project. By offering to compromise or provide an alternative option, you're softening the refusal and still helping the other person. That way, you'll both come out of the discussion feeling that your needs were heard and respected, and a solution was found.

Show Gratitude

No always sounds better when you remember to use it with an expression of thanks. "It's nice of you to ask, but I'm afraid I'm not available that weekend" sounds so much better than just "I'm not available that weekend." Again, be sincere in your expression. This is an especially valuable tool to use when you're anxious to avoid burning bridges with an individual because you want to work with them sometime in the future.

Don't Over-Apologize

Anytime you apologize, you're putting yourself in a weaker position that makes it sound like you either want to be asked again or are open to being badgered into accepting. "I'm sorry" tends to sound wishy-washy, like you really regret not being able to say yes. This will sometimes be interpreted as you saying, "Convince me" rather than "No, thank you." Instead, express your no in a firm and confident tone of voice. Don't be sorry, don't express regret. Just say no in simple terms. If the person still keeps asking, express the no as many times as it takes to get the point across. Keep in mind that you can always walk away, especially if someone is badgering you.

Soften Your Language

No is about being in control, not expressing dominance. There's a fine distinction. When saying no, be kind and respectful. Try the "sandwich" approach by saying something positive, then saying no, then finishing with something positive. Something along the lines of "That sounds like a great project. While I can't help you with that, I appreciate your thinking of me" works perfectly.

ACT NOW · 239

Refer to Your Commitment to Others

When you're overbooked, it should be easy to say no outright, but sometimes it can still be a challenge. Sticking with honesty once again (see a trend here?), if you are already doing things for other people, let the person asking you know that. Just politely and firmly tell them you currently have too many other people relying on you to take on any more commitments.

Confine Your Feelings

No matter what you do, you're going to want to rein in your emotions. This isn't the time or place to get upset. The more emotional you are, the more likely your refusal will turn into that conflict that you were trying so hard to avoid. Do what you can to keep things level and unemotional. Take a few deep breaths and remember this doesn't have to be personal. Are you still having trouble? If so, step back until you can rein in your emotions. Tell the other person that you need a minute, or ask if you can get back to them tomorrow. That gives you the space and time you need to separate yourself emotionally from the situation so that you can provide a calm and clear no.

Realize That Saying No Isn't Always About Only You

Sometimes the best approach is to step back from the situation entirely. Sometimes you aren't saying no just because of your own schedule. Sometimes you are acting as a representative of a company or a family. This keeps the no from feeling personal and takes a situation away from "I am not able to make that commitment to you" and over to "Our company is not able to make that commitment to you." By acting as a representative, you can gain some much-needed emotional distance from what might be an uncomfortable situation.

Practice

As with anything, saying no gets easier the more you do it. It might seem daunting at first, especially if you're not wired that way, but trust us, it gets easier. The more you commit to setting your personal boundaries by saying no, the better you will get at it. Once you're more comfortable with saying no, you will wonder why you weren't doing it more often before! Soon, you'll find that you're able to embrace the no and use it in your life to regain power and control where you never had any previously. This is a fantastic feeling and one that will help you to progress in ways that you never dreamed you could. Any new skill needs hours of reinforcement for it to become a habit. Building your just-say-no muscles will make it easier to stick to your decisions and not be tempted to give in. Those muscles are important to help you maintain your boundaries. Make sure you keep them toned and strong!

Having healthy boundaries is a fine art. Therefore,

mastering the valuable skill of knowing when to say yes and no makes you an artist, a visionary, and a person of power. That might seem a little over the top, but think about it. Before you said no, what were you? Now, with these skills under your belt, you're able to not only see the future but also plan for it. You've learned the fine art of improving your relationships with those around you, and you've managed to take charge of your life.

I (Natalie) experienced other lessons along the way, but what I have learned from these lessons are those points and practices I need to be aware of to be able in order to walk away faster, not look back, and try not to allow history to repeat itself. I learned to leave negative environments behind. I learned to leave anything that would stall me or weigh me down on the side of the road. I learned to make a leap so that the world around me would pause and I could gain focus.

I learned to be open to see and hear signs telling me to get out. I also learned that you don't have to say yes to everything; it is ok to say no. Further, Reg flat-out asked me about my core values. She taught me that if something does not align with my core values and push me in the direction I need to be going, it makes the decision easy, and I didn't need to feel badly about it, especially if the answer is no.

Furthermore, no is a complete sentence. You don't have to explain your no.

CREATING YOUR OWN POWER

Not being able to refuse is disempowering. It's offering to be a doormat to whoever comes along next! You may as well put up a sign saying, "Your needs before mine." If you often feel pressured to be a people-pleaser, learning to say no will release you from needing others' approval to boost your self-esteem. Saying no to others' demands means saying yes to yourself. Learning to say no is a decisive act in taking back your power because you are declaring what's important in your life. You are setting your agenda and acting on it. Putting yourself first and saying no sometimes means you are asserting your right to have your needs met before you can meet the needs of others. That sends a powerful message about your place in the world. It signals a strong honest person who is secure in knowing and respecting their own needs, not a "doormat."

In saying no, you can take back those expectations and the power that comes with doing so. You start with setting your own boundaries, then maintaining them. If you become known as that person who won't work on Saturday because that's your day with the family, eventually people will just quit asking. They will come to realize that the answer is always going to be no on Saturdays. What's more, this becomes part of who you are. The world around you becomes aware of your boundaries and knows that you're a person who sticks to your word. If you say no to certain kinds of things, expectations form. It becomes obvious that there's no point in even asking you if you're going to say no. This further protects you from frivolous time-wasting requests. It will also lead to you being admired for your integrity and always sticking to what you believe in.

THE PROBLEM WITH NOT HAVING BOUNDARIES

As mentioned before, the more you say yes, the more packed your schedule gets. The more packed your schedule, the more overwhelming it can be. Especially when you find that you tend to say yes to the point where your downtime suffers. Before you know it, you can't even remember when you last had a minute to yourself, and that's not healthy. The problem with living under this kind of constant stress is that sooner or later your body will tell you that enough is enough. This is where you start seeing problems: weight gain from grabbing too many quick meals, high blood pressure from constant deadlines, poor sleep at night—all because you're worried about how you're going to get it all done. All this adds up very quickly. Keep it up, and you can be assured of a quick trip to the doctor or even the hospital at some point. While that's guaranteed to clear your schedule, it won't be in the way that you want.

So, how do you get on top of things? You start by protecting your commitment level. When you were a child, you might have been criticized for putting too much food on your plate. You might have even been told that "your eyes are bigger than your stomach." It's a great saying that reminds us that we too often overestimate our abilities. Only this time, we're not talking about food, but instead the level of work you can take on. We forget to build in that cushion just in case the project takes a little longer. Or, we convince ourselves that we can do the project in less time than we should. We think we actually do have time in our schedule for that extra project when our to-do list is trying desperately to tell us otherwise.

Whatever has caused you to become over-committed and to have more than you can manage, you should stop to determine how best to resolve the issue. Start by cutting yourself some slack. If you want to take on something new, great! But, be sure to be reasonable in assessing the amount of time that it's going to take. Sit down and evaluate this point honestly. Is this a weekly commitment? Daily? What kind of deadline is already attached? Is that feasible? Estimate how long you think a project will take, and then build in a little extra time just in case something comes up. Also, be reasonable about your current workload. If you already have more than enough to do, it's probably time to say no. After all, you can't do everything, no matter how hard you try.

PRIORITIZE YOURSELF

For some of us, this might be the hardest concept to grasp. To understand the importance of taking care of your own needs first, you're going to have to accept that you have value, and that your needs are essential. If you have trouble wrapping your mind around this, you might be a "people pleaser." People pleasers tend to put the needs of others before their own. Why? A lot of times, it stems from childhood. Somewhere along the way, we were taught that thinking about ourselves first was selfish. We also find out that doing things for other people makes them happy with us. This need to please becomes so ingrained in us that we carry the concept into adulthood.

As adults, we frequently forget that it's impossible to take care of the needs of anyone else if or our own needs aren't met first. You can't work if you're so hungry that you're lost in a brain fog. You're never going to meet your deadline if you're so exhausted that you can't finish that report. If you forget to exercise, eventually your body will let you know that it doesn't have the energy for one more commitment. You have to realize that you really can't give your best when you aren't at your best. This is when you need to learn how to say no for the so-called selfish reasons. Make saying no a positive decision that allows more you time into your schedule. You decide what you need to do to protect yourself so that you can answer yes to the things that matter. This means things like:

- Not letting random requests interfere with your workout regimen
- Making sure you don't skip meals to honor a request
- Ensuring that that you do get enough sleep and downtime

"Self-care is giving the world the best of you, instead of what's left of you."
—**Katie Reed**

Having a successful mindset also begins with how you take care of yourself and how you are able to look at yourself and believe in yourself. Confidence comes from being comfortable in your own skin and the way you look, which translates into how you feel and how you are able to bring out your unique qualities when combining your voice with that of your company's brand.

It is important to have routines in place and goals to reach, not only in business but also in your overall health and wellness. The better you feel, the more energy you will have to do what you need to do in your business and life. It starts with taking care of you. Exercising and eating well feeds your body and your mind with what you need.

Did you know the average age of an entrepreneur

is forty? According to studies out of Duke University, the Kauffman Foundation, the Founder Institute, and Northwestern, the average entrepreneur is forty years old when launching his or her first startup—and the average age of leaders of high-growth startups is *forty-five.*

Both Reg and I are at an age where you either stay where you are, pursuing the career that you think you are supposed to because it is what you studied in school or what you trained for, or you choose to do something new and exciting because you know that it is something you are excited about—and it aligns with what is important to you. Chances are, it may even be your purpose. It is people like us, and probably you, who at some point decide to jump into the entrepreneurial experience.

As more people decide to become entrepreneurs, they are finding themselves working more hours than ever before. When you have an employer, there is an established paycheck distributed on a given payday in exchange for work outcomes and expectations. And, while jobs can be stressful, especially if they are very demanding, you are able to establish clearer boundaries. When you work for yourself, the buck stops with you. If you don't put in whatever number of hours are needed to meet your revenue goals, everything stops. This can take a huge toll on your mental and physical existence.

The body has a way of letting you know what its

limits are. You may hustle and grind in an effort to keep things afloat, but your body will start to take charge and command attention if not given adequate attention and balance. If you are not mindful of the demands that you place on yourself, it can take a toll on your energy, your physical existence, and even your thought processes. Some enter into the entrepreneurial experience much older than age forty, and sometimes they feel as though they've entered this game too late or are too old to start something so new and different. This couldn't be further from the truth. However, it is extremely important, at any age, to take care of your mind and body. Maintain healthy boundaries and balance between your work and personal life. Remember to be good to your body, and it will be good to you. Clarity comes from feeding the entire body with good health!

Nineteenth-century Danish philosopher Soren Kierkegaard, in a letter to his niece, wrote, "Above all, do not lose your desire to walk…every day I walk myself into a state of well-being and walk away from every illness. I have walked myself into my best thoughts…Health and salvation can only be found in motion."

Physical activity and exercise have been lauded for their positive effects on the body, but physicians and researchers have become more interested in the effects on brain health and cognition. Based on recent findings, the hippocampus (the part of our brain that regulates emotion, motivation, learning, and memory) could be especially sensitive to the effects of exercise.[1] The benefits of exercise (specifically aerobic exercise) are many. Simply increasing heart rate pumps more blood to the brain, increasing the flow of oxygen and hormones to brain cells. Exercise can even stimulate new connections between brain cells.[2]

As much as exercise helps the brain, there is also a strong connection between both sleep quantity and quality and the potential for cognitive decline. Throughout the day, our brains produce a type of protein called amyloid plaques. These plaques can accumulate in some of the space between brain cells and can be harmful if they continue to build up. Abnormally high levels of amyloid plaques are a distinguishing trademark of Alzheimer's disease and are present with certain types of dementia.[3] During a "good night's sleep" (seven to nine hours for adults and nine to eleven hours for teens and adolescents)[4] your brain has time to "clean out" these potentially damaging proteins that have built up during the day. While you are sleeping, the flow of cerebrospinal fluid increases significantly, almost literally washing away these harmful proteins.[5]

Finally, your diet also plays a role in preserving brain health and minimizing memory loss. Dietary practices that are high in sugar, refined carbohydrates, unhealthy fats, and processed foods can negatively affect memory and learning.

Just like anything else, make small goals to work on the inside and reap the benefits from the energy that comes with good health and a clear mind.

This could be a walk for twenty to thirty minutes, choosing to eat healthy and reducing sugar and processed foods.

But you can't stop there. While physical health is important, your mental health is equally important. Learning to say no will reduce the amount of stress in your life. Think of how your body reacts when you feel pressured to say yes to something you don't want to do, or when you can't see how you can fit one more thing into your schedule. Does your stomach tense? Does your throat tighten? Does your heartbeat increase? The stress of being a people-pleaser can be actively bad for your health, raising your blood pressure and bodily inflammation while reducing your immune system. If you're overburdened because you can't refuse people, it's likely you'll be lying awake worrying about how you're going to get everything done. There are enough stresses in your life already without adding to them. Make the firm decision now to take control and eliminate as many of those stresses as you can. Learn to make saying no a positive habit in your life, and watch your stress levels drop! Doing things that tear down your self-esteem, that send you into a spiral of self-hate and resentment, will eventually turn into bigger issues. It's nearly impossible to be productive when you're struggling emotionally just to get through the day. So, what can you do? Start saying no to things that will leave you burned out and emotionally exhausted. Some people or projects are drains on your mental resources. You're no good to anyone else if you neglect to protect your mental health.

When you learn to say no clearly, politely and firmly, you feel better and have more time to focus on the things you want to do. Also, all the people who are currently sucking the energy out of you with their demands will melt away. Everyone encounters energy vampires from time to time—those people who don't seem to do anything but take, take, take, and then take some more. Whether it's the soccer mom who expects you to ferry her kids around, the family member who never hosts a get-together, or the office leech who ducks responsibility all the time, you'll find toxic people everywhere. They never make you feel good, and they won't leave you alone until you learn to say no. Energy vampires are masters of manipulation and emotional blackmail. They're also known for gaslighting and leaving you in the lurch. Make up your mind to see them for what they are, consistently and firmly say no. Keep saying it until they're gone. Saying no is kryptonite for energy vampires!

If working with someone is bad for your mental and emotional health, it seriously is time to say no—quickly. **This is perhaps one of the most important boundaries you'll ever set, and probably**

the one that will give you back the most power over your life.

PRIORITIZE PEOPLE YOU REALLY CARE ABOUT

Why are you saying yes to people who don't even matter? Here's one of the worst problems about saying yes all the time—we become indiscriminate about who we say yes to. This means that every request becomes equally important. Should that be the case? No! Saying no means taking back the ability to decide who it is we want to work with and who we want to support. It means that not everyone is equal in importance in your life, and you get to decide who is—and isn't. This is an amazingly powerful feeling. You start by establishing more boundaries. When you receive a request from someone, remind yourself who is doing the asking. Is this someone you like and respect? Can you work with them either way? Sometimes you're not given a choice in terms of who you work with, but If you have some flexibility, you might want to look into other options.

Working with people you don't like is quite emotionally draining—even physically. You'll get tired more quickly and won't be as productive. When a request means you might have to deal with a difficult person, a solution might mean offering a no, but with an alternative. For example: Maybe you don't get along with some of the other parents in the parent-teacher organization at your child's school. You might decide that serving on a committee with those individuals would be too much of a headache. But, you have no problem at all volunteering with the kids on Sports Day. This creates a compromise that you can live with while allowing you to be part of your child's life at school.

You might be surprised to hear that saying no will improve your relationships with colleagues, family, and friends. After all, that notion flies in the face of all the messages you probably got from your mom when you were growing up, and still get from society. Surely, saying no and putting yourself first is selfish, and other people won't like you anymore, right? Maybe you won't get promoted, or you'll lose friends. The opposite is true. Learning to say no effectively and politely means being clear and honest about your needs and your boundaries. That's rare in today's world. Chances are, you'll find that people appreciate your honesty and will respect you for it. Remember that a good relationship ought not to be transactional. People love or like you for who you are, not for what you can do for them. And if they can't accept that, maybe you're better off without them in your life.

REDUCE FRUSTRATION

Frustration is a part of life. We all have to deal with it from time to time. But, what if we could reduce it by simply saying no? Nothing is quite so frustrating as being taken for granted. After a while, you can't help but think that if you didn't jump up and say yes to everything, no one would ever see you at all.

Worse, when you say no, you tend to prove that very point. Often, people who needed us just seconds earlier forget we exist after hearing no. Sometimes, no matter how many times you've said yes to someone else, you're still the one hearing no when you need something done.

The quickest way to lower our frustration is to cut the dead weight out of our life. This means getting rid of those projects and people that you find frustrating. Why are you putting yourself through emotional distress for someone who doesn't appreciate you in the first place? Start by looking at what is being asked of you. How does the request make you feel? If you've got resentment and frustration building before you so much as open your mouth, it's time to say no.

Those feelings are only going to build and grow worse over time. The longer you're on the project, the more you're likely to regret it. Saying no from the outset eliminates all that frustration right from the start. The interesting side effect of saying no is that you're more apt to be both noticed and respected when you do. When you say no, you're telling the world that you have value and worth, and that you respect yourself enough to put your needs first. Not to mention, the very fact that you're able to confidently say no once in a while gives your yes that much more value. After all, who would you rather hang out with—the person who says yes to absolutely everything or the one who has chosen to say yes to you alone?

Don't feel like you're there yet? You will be. Keep in mind that all this change isn't going to happen overnight. New skills take time to master, and as is true with any habit, the more the practice saying no, the better you'll get at it. Slipping up and saying yes to the wrong thing isn't going to be the end of the world. Just take note of the event and learn from it. This way, the next time that situation comes up, you'll know better how to handle it.

Try to remember these three important things:

1. Saying no is a positive and powerful experience.
2. Recognizing when to say no is half the battle.
3. Saying no doesn't have to be difficult.

Embrace the life that saying no has given you. You're powerful. You're in control. Now go accomplish great things!

Chapter Review

- Healthy boundaries consider the ability to assess and identify both time and energy and how to protect both.

- No is a boundary line. It defines the edge between us and the world and protects us.
- Knowing that no is powerful and knowing when to use it are often two very different things.
- Protect your commitment level by pausing and evaluating commitments reasonably and honestly.
- Understanding the importance of taking care of your own needs starts with the acceptance that you have value and your needs are essential.
- Change isn't going to happen overnight. New skills take time to master, and with any habit, the more the practice, the better you'll get.

Time to ACT!

Today's Date:

Assess – Journal about what you wish to take action on related to this chapter's topic.

Commit – Write down the action you are willing to commit to in the next twelve months.

Transform – Identify an actionable goal that will transform the commitment into a measurable outcome.

CHAPTER TWELVE

BE STILL AND KNOW (MINDFULNESS)

"You must learn to master a new way to think before you can master a new way to be."
—Marianne Williamson

I (Natalie) always pause when I think about mindfulness. People ask me all the time if I meditate or do yoga. Part of me quickly thinks, "I don't have time to be quiet." But when I do force myself to be quiet and actively mindful, I make leaps and bounds into the next step of my journey. So why do I still think that I don't have the time or that it isn't important?

This is one of my goals—to focus on things more intently, eliminating distractions and saying no to things that do not align with my goals, core values, and beliefs. I truly believe that the more I can focus on being present in what I am working on or who I am working with, the better-quality connection I will make, and the swifter and more efficient action I will be able to take.

Many of the ways to practice mindfulness are not be for everyone, but if you can choose at least some ways that you can pause life, I am sure you will reap the benefits, as there is much power in the pause.

It is important to understand that you can command your own thoughts, and your thoughts can determine your environment. This a significant step in learning to be a person of action. However, learning to commit to a daily routine of developing mental and emotional strength is something else entirely. It takes discipline, character, and a great deal of patience. We are able to manifest things, but believing that we can manifest anything we want is misguided. As human beings, we are creators. Creation starts in the mind. If you think about it, we can't cause anything to occur without first having a thought about it; all actions must first start with a thought. However, the thought must eventually translate to actions if any tangible results are to be seen.

The problem that we often face in moving from thoughts to actions is distraction. Distractions can come disguised in many forms: fear, doubt, lack, and overwhelm, for starters. Our minds are bombarded with random thoughts on a regular basis. Besides being interesting, understanding how these three areas of the brain function and impact our thoughts helps us to understand why quieting the mind is a challenge at best.

It is challenging to be creative these days because we are often unable to settle our minds long enough to block out all of the internal and external stimuli that prevents us from creating, visualizing, and then establishing plans to take action.

We need to make sure we do not spend time focusing on worry, stress, eating foods that are not good for us, staying involved in toxic relationships, and operating in limiting belief systems. These are just some of the contributing factors to our inability to quiet ourselves and focus on mindfulness. Learning strategies to quiet the mind and become mindful is critical to becoming a person of action.

Below are some suggested areas of mindfulness that you might consider practicing:

Meditation

Meditation is a great practice for mental development. It involves sitting quietly and being observant of movements within the mind.

Taking the time to meditate involves just that: time. After a period of time, the mind automatically starts to quiet down and become less frantic and more focused. You become less reactive to outside events and are able to monitor and control your thoughts much more effectively and efficiently.

Vipassana and Transcendental Meditation are two of the most popular kinds of meditation. Both methods have an extensive body of scientific literature that pertain to their use and benefits. It can be quite simple to implement a regular meditation routine, and it is an important step, as it is verified by science, practiced by many high-achieving individuals, and even has historic roots in spiritual ecosystems.

For the best results, it is recommended to consider a twice-a-day routine for twenty minutes in the morning and evening. In some cases, you can also consider a more intense course for a week to really kick-off your practice.

Yoga

Yoga is a practice of movements of the body that involve the breath, concentration, flexibility, balance, and physical strength. When the particular movements are executed in a certain routine and fashion, over time the person who participates can arrive into a state of flow and balance, and is eventually able to complete an hour-long routine effortlessly. Yoga also incorporates the coordination of exact breathing, concentration, and physical exertion, which—when practiced together and mindfully—are perfect for subduing the mind. Yoga is not possible to effectively perform with an active mind, as it gets in the way. In addition, yoga is best practiced when it becomes a regular habit that does not require conscious thought.

Fasting

Though many believe fasting is both described and practiced as a pretty extreme method, it's one of the best ways to help master your mind. We are so connected to food; it is more important to a human being than anything else. Therefore, giving up food for a significant period of time takes incredible willpower, but it has many benefits. In addition, research shows that fasting is the one thing that has been proven to increase longevity in rats, and although difficult to believe for many of us, humans actually perform best when they are just a little hungry. There are different ways to fast. Some are not based on food or sustenance, such as a water fast, a juice fast, even a dry fast. One way to start fasting could be considering a three-day juice or sugar fast once a month for both an emotional and mental detox.

Mindfulness

Mindfulness can take on many forms, and there is a plethora of mindfulness practices. Being mindful involves being aware at regular intervals throughout the day. Mindfulness can even be combined with meditation for greater results. While meditating, we are able to sit deeply and be "non-focused" for twenty to thirty minutes, twice a day. In addition to meditation, we are able to add awareness with mindfulness, which allows us to focus on specific things at periods throughout our day. Mindfulness is often linked with breathing, as it can be a quick route to the present moment. Therefore, if you have a desk job and you leave your desk every forty minutes and, during that time, are mindful of your breathing for just a single minute, it can help you detach from your tasks.

Concentration

Concentration involves time and technique. There are many types of concentration techniques available. Some include focusing on a candle flame for a few minutes a day, focusing on the top of your nose, or focusing on your breath. Many spiritual practitioners recommend spending no more than ten minutes of intense concentration on anything. Ten minutes is coincidentally the maximum amount of time that a human being can focus intensely on anything, according to scientific research.

Practices of Passion and Intensity

If you are able to focus on the things that you are really passionate about, you will be able to continue to focus on them with single-minded intensity. This can include painting, dancing, singing, martial arts, creating a business or organization from an idea, or really anything to which you are able to give 100 percent of your mental attention. This is helpful because you will not have the time to energize negative thoughts or emotions surrounding you, as all of your resources will be aimed towards one particular activi-

ACT NOW · 265

ty. Focus is one of the most effective ways to control the mind and remove any destructive tendencies. Unless you are really passionate about something, it can be very difficult to develop your concentration and willpower in order to see it through. This is why most people give up their resolutions too soon.

ADVANCED PROTOCOLS

In some cases, there are strategies you can use if you really want to be able to gain control over the mind. They are designed so that you will make breakthroughs that can lead to long-term gain. Consider a one- to two-week silent retreat in a quiet and serene location, possibly out in nature, without many of your daily distractions and technology. During this silent retreat, you would be able to meditate and sit in a quiet space to facilitate focus twice a day, complete a yoga or low-impact exercise routine, and stick to a healthy and whole foods diet without alcohol, sugar, or processed foods.

If you are able to stick to a routine, you will definitely see the benefit for a number of reasons. A silent retreat brings the observation of contrast and goes against the insanity and noise of the everyday environment. When you reintroduce yourself into your everyday environment as well as reintroduce certain foods back into your diet, the outlook with which you made previous decisions will be apparent. It is a great idea to aim for a practice of retreat and reflection every three months in order to reconnect. This type of practice will assist you in better navigating the normal and sometimes even chaotic work environment to better achieve a peaceful state of being.

Affirmations

Affirmations are an effective tool to re-program ourselves for both business and personal success. It is important to remember when employing affirmations to use the present tense, such as "I am skilled" or "I am successful," which are better than "I will be skilled or "I am going to be successful." Another point to keep top of mind is that affirmations work best when the mind is in a receptive state. Affirmations should be stated first thing in the morning or late at night. Another great time to repeat your affirmations is while meditating, when they can really sink in without any resistance.

Affirmations can work, but they have to be repeated so that our subconscious can receive the message loud and clear. For the best results, they need to be stated either internally or out loud. It should also be understood that some people have deep convictions with regard to money, love, and even sexuality. In some cases, an individual may not believe that they are worthy of love or affection. In this instance, affirmations may not work, and self-examination, diet, yoga, and meditation might be needed to alter the person's mindset into a more positive state.

In other cases, therapists are involved in hypnotizing patients, with their consent, into a more positive belief system. After a while, however, the underlying negative belief can reemerge. This can suggest that the belief is further rooted, or that it comes from somewhere even deeper than the subconscious mind. Sometimes, combining both affirmations with meditation achieves better results. Some people can create and develop their affirmations into a poem that rhymes, which allows for improved recall. The subconscious will then be able to repeat it consistently, much like a when a song gets stuck in your head. Making that connection is one of the best ways to get rid of a limiting belief. If and when possible, try to see if you are able to feel the affirmation as a positive emotion. This may help supercharge it with energy into manifestation.

Did you know there are available online tests to see where you have limiting beliefs? They may be circling around self-love, money, relationships, abundance, or happiness. Once you are able to define where the limiting beliefs lie, you can create affirmations that surround those beliefs and use different terms and tenses to navigate around the beliefs more rapidly.

For example:

"I am enough."

"I am joyful."

"I live a life of abundance."

"I am successful in achieving my dreams."

"I have the power within to do anything I desire."

"I can generate the income that I desire."

"When someone tells me no, it is not a reflection of my abilities."

"Money is a tool to allow me to do good in the world."

"I am filled with great purpose."

"My purpose is important."

In general, with affirmations it is better to use present tense and avoid negative statements such as "I am not in poverty." The brain is not able to distinguish between real and imaginary, therefore it also does not understand negation. All it hears is "poverty."

Self-Programming Strategies
There are many strategies you can apply to self-program your mind. The best times for self-

programming is usually when you are just waking as well as when you are settling down to sleep. Meditation is another great time to focus on ways to change.

As much as possible, you still need to use the rest of the day to place yourself into a positive state of mind. If you work at a desk job, you may also be stuck sitting and on a computer for at least eight hours a day. In order to make the most of your situation and environment, try to listen to music for a couple of hours a day. Sometimes music that does not have any patterns or meaning is a good choice. Binaural beats and theta brainwave tracks are available on You Tube and other sites and apps. In addition, try recording yourself speaking empowering affirmations, and then listen to it for a period of time. Subconsciously, affirmative statements such as "I am rich," "I am intelligent," and "I am attractive" will begin to stick and start to manifest in your everyday life.

You could also consider seeing a therapist or lucid dreaming as a means of accessing the subconscious. Again, there are a large number of self-programming strategies available. It is important to focus and try to pick one or two and stick with them for a consistent length of time.

Chapter Review

- Understanding that your thoughts can determine your environment and that you can further com-

mand your thoughts is learning to be a person of action.
- With affirmations, it is better to use the present tense and avoid negative statements.
- The best times to engage in self-programming are just after waking and when settling down to sleep.

Time to ACT!

Today's Date:

Assess – Journal about what you wish to take action on related to this chapter's topic.

Commit – Write down the action you are willing to commit to in the next twelve months.

Transform – Identify an actionable goal that will transform the commitment into a measurable outcome.

CLOSING

We decided to write this book together for many reasons. We are both entrepreneurs and are driven by an important desire to give back to the world in a positive way. We have many ideas, have learned to pivot, continue to create, and love problem-solving. Although we are both successful in our own businesses, for years we've known that there was more inside of us individually, as well as together as a team. The powerful passion and purpose that lived inside both of us could have lived as an ember inside each of us long before it became a burning flame. However, we knew that our friendship and discipline would lead us to keeping each other accountable, knowing that each of us had so much more to give.

The biggest step was committing to each other and working together in order to evolve and challenge ourselves to be better, bigger, and brighter.

Through this book and our work, we want to share what we've learned with others, especially those who might be feeling stuck. It is our hope that this book will spark a movement of people taking action on their greatest goals and dreams and help them feel confident in doing so. We want to encourage everyone to utilize the power of momentum to start taking action. Newton's First Law of Motion states that a body in motion stays in motion, and a body at rest stays at rest, unless acted upon by an outside force. We aim to be that outside force that is the catalyst to your positive action.

To get you started in moving towards action, we want you to consider where you may have been stuck up until now, and apply the following steps:

Recognize the Problem

You know that something needs to change because things aren't working. The question is, are you happy here where you are, or do you want to move forward? This question becomes important because, in some areas, we really might be happier with the status quo. After all, there's no challenge in keeping things the same. On the other hand, it's also a quick way to become stagnant. If this doesn't sound appealing, take a minute to acknowledge what exactly is going on and then do yourself a favor and ditch the excuses. Make a commitment to yourself to do what needs to be done in order to go after what's important to you.

Take a Step Back

You know what needs changing, but do you know why? Understanding the reasons why you are holding back or allowing something else to get in the way is important, especially if you intend to get moving again. Did something come up that seemed (or actually is) more important? Does something about the process seem hard? Are you dealing with old baggage? Whatever the case, you can't move forward without understanding where you are now. Don't forget to address the most important question of all: What do you actually want to be doing right now? Have your goals changed?

Reconsider

You might have gleaned a hint of this from the last step. Ask yourself what the most important thing to you is right now. What is the logical next step? Do you need to reconsider the goal? Or, perhaps you want to change the way you're going about trying to achieve it. Explore your life's purpose and spend time reviewing your core values and mission statement if it helps. While the last step was about the why of things, this step is about looking at the what. You might also want to include in this step consideration of whether there are things weighing down your purpose. What do you need to remove from your life that is currently acting as an anchor holding you in place?

Build a Road Map

Now, with a clearer purpose, it's time to figure out a plan of attack. With a clarified goal and a new sense of purpose, you're ready to think about strategy. Remember, deliberately setting a course of action is more conducive to achieving success than acting randomly on whatever task seems best in the moment. Setting this course of action needs to include small steps, tasks you can perform every single day so you can start building back your momentum. It's important to keep goals small; otherwise, it's easy to become discouraged when there's too much on your plate. If that happens, you'll likely lose momentum all over again.

Remember that, throughout the book, we have been encouraging you to follow our simple three-step process to ACT: (1) Assess where you are, (2) Commit to a plan, and (3) Transform your life through the execution of the plan. If you applied this system to each area discussed within the book, you should now have specific areas in which you are taking action and a plan with solid strategies to get you closer to achieving your goals and dreams.

We are so thankful for the journey you have decided to take in reading our book, and hope it has provided a guide for you to ACT Now! Our greatest hope is that it helps lead you to the steps needed to reach and accomplish your dreams. We believe that one of the earliest steps to ACT begins with your own decision to step up, identify what success looks like for you, and establishing a goal-centered plan to help you reach that success. Almost immediately, the very next step is to connect to someone who can help to keep you accountable in your journey.

We want you to know, you are never alone. We truly believe that an authentic connection is needed through a community of people who want nothing more than to help you move forward on your plan. We would love to be able to help guide you into making that connection and keep you focused on your journey. If you have made the decision to ACT Now, please connect with us on social media, and visit our website at www.actnowguide.com to join our community of ACTion Takers!

About the Authors

REGEANIE CORONA

Regeanie Corona is a business development strategist, nonprofit specialist, speaker, trainer, and purpose life coach with over thirty years of experience in Information Technology, Business Systems Development and Integration, Business Development, Strategic Planning, and training/development in both the public and private sectors. She has managed multimillion-dollar projects and has helped to raise over $6.5M in support of community development, economic development and public health-related projects benefiting underserved individuals.

Driven by a desire to help others thrive in life and business, she now assists current and aspiring nonprofit leaders and social entrepreneurs wishing to achieve maximum efficiency in running and growing their operations. With more than seventeen years of leadership experience, she has also learned to utilize her skills to help organizations from multiple sectors come together in collaborative partnerships to build strong and healthy communities.

Regeanie is the Founder and CEO of Advancing The Seed, Inc., a 501(c)3 nonprofit organization based in Southern California, whose mission is to develop strong leaders for business and community engagement.

www.Regeanie.com

DR. NATALIE PHILLIPS

Dr. Natalie Phillips is passionate about building deep relationships and authentic connections to help make a difference in the world. She is committed to assisting individuals and businesses to become more of who they are and to live out their brand. She believes in creating environments in which people can connect on different levels to help their businesses succeed.

She is the founder and CEO of Connect4Excellence, LLC, a company dedicated to guide individuals, entrepreneurs, and businesses to connect to their own mission and culture; to connect to others at organized events; to connect to their own voice with a bigger audience on social media; and to connect in order to give back and create social impact. She is the host of "Connecting A Better World," a podcast aimed to connect people to listen, learn, and spark interest in how they see what they can bring forth to make this world a better place.

Dr. Phillips is also a Senior Audiologist with Advanced Otolaryngology and Audiology in Fort Collins, Colorado. She's the co-host of a weekly Facebook Live show, "All Things AuD" and you can join in the conversation with Dr. Phillips every Thursday at 12:30pm MST to discuss and learn about topics on ears, hearing, hearing technology, tinnitus, sound sensitivity, and balance disorders. In addition to seeing patients and diagnosing and treating hearing loss, tinnitus, and balance disorders of the ear, being involved in research and on clinical advisory boards, she has volunteered her time to travel overseas to India, Peru, Guyana, and Mexico as well as served in the United States as a Global Hearing Ambassador to deliver the gift of hearing with the Starkey Hearing Foundation by fitting hearing aids on people who are unable to afford the technology.

https://drnatalie-phillips.com

Made in the USA
Coppell, TX
01 October 2020

39044868R00173